The Foundations of
Socratic Ethics

The Foundations of Socratic Ethics

Alfonso Gómez-Lobo

Hackett Publishing Company, Inc.
Indianapolis/Cambridge

Printed in the United States of America

00 99 98 97 96 95 94   1 2 3 4 5 6 7

For further information, please address

Hackett Publishing Company, Inc.
P.O. Box 44937
Indianapolis, Indiana 46244-0937

Design by Dan Kirklin

Library of Congress Cataloging-in-Publication Data

Gómez-Lobo, Alfonso, 1940–
    [Etica de Sócrates. English]
    The foundations of Socratic ethics/Alfonso Gómez-Lobo.
        p.   cm.
    Includes bibliographical references and index.
    ISBN 0-87220-174-0.
    1. Socrates—Ethics.   2. Plato.   I. Title.
B318.E8G6513 1994
170'.92—dc20   94–25963
                                                            CIP

The paper used in this publication meets the minimum requirements of American National Standard for Information Sciences—Permanence of Paper for Printed Library Materials, ANSI Z39.48-1984.

∞

Contents

To the memory of
Gregory Vlastos

The Foundations of
Socratic Ethics

Foreword

This book was originally written in Spanish in 1986. It appeared in 1989 in Mexico under the title *La ética de Sócrates*. Its aim was to offer beginners and nonspecialists an account of the moral philosophy underlying some of the early Platonic dialogues.

In its present form this introductory book is essentially the author's translation of the original version. The passage of time, however, and excellent recent scholarship on Socrates have prompted second thoughts on some issues. This made some rewriting unavoidable. Moreover, the privilege of being one's own translator creates a unique opportunity to depart from the original without committing an act of treason. I have thus felt free to introduce changes and to omit information that is readily available to readers of English.

In the first version of the book, I tried to steer away from detailed scholarly controversy in order to reach the kind of audience at which the work is aimed. This is also a feature of the current version. The references in the notes to the sources and to selected items in the secondary literature should enable more advanced readers to further pursue their own study of Socratic ethics. Beginners would be well advised to disregard them.

Although extensive use was made of research published by earlier generations of scholars, I owe a special debt of gratitude to books and papers by Gregory Vlastos, Gerasimos Santas, and Charles Kahn. This, of course, does not imply that they would necessarily agree with anything held in the pages that follow.

In fact, I remain painfully aware of the many shortcomings of the book, among them the almost complete silence on the connections between drama and philosophy in the Platonic writings. Parsimony and brevity have their price.

Most of the research and writing was made possible by a leave of absence from Georgetown University in the spring of 1986 and by a generous fellowship from the John S. Guggenheim Foundation, New York. Jorge and Charo Echenique provided me with an ideal setting for study, reflection, and writing in their beautiful house in Santiago, Chile.

I am grateful to Professor Héctor Carvallo of the University of Chile, who gave me access to his private library and was willing to share with me his admirable knowledge of the sources of Greek philosophy, most of it acquired when we were fellow students in Munich several decades ago.

My gratitude is extended to the anonymous readers for Hackett Publishing Company who made many valuable observations (including the suggestion of a new, more accurate title).

I would also like to thank Jeffrey Jennings, Deborah Wilkes, and the staff of Hackett for their patience and their help in the preparation of the manuscript.

It is fitting that this little book be dedicated to the memory of Professor Vlastos. It is to him that I owe the suggestion and encouragement to make it available in English.

Last but not least, my gratitude also goes to Jimena, my wife, without whose love and patience this book would not exist in any of its versions.

Washington, D.C.
March 1994

Introduction

In the spring of 399 B.C., when he was about to be executed by the Athenian state, Socrates was offered the opportunity to escape from jail and avoid drinking the hemlock. He refused.

His decision may be judged in different ways. To some, it was simply foolish not to accept the offer, especially given his claim to have been unjustly condemned to death.

Alternatively, one can interpret Socrates' choice as an attempt on his part to do his moral duty, at great personal cost, by refusing to violate Athenian law. Indeed, many people, both in fifth-century Athens and now, would agree that a person who follows the dictates of morality will often be required to do something opposed to self-interest. Moral integrity seems to conflict with the pursuit of one's own good, and ultimately of one's own happiness.

Socrates appears to have radically opposed the view that such a conflict exists. This made him an oddity among his contemporaries and an intriguing figure for us. How did Socrates view the connections between self-interest and morality? In exploring his views, this book reveals the foundations of an admirably coherent conception of ethics, a conception—as we shall see—that defies classification into the currently favored categories of ethical theories (divine command, deontological, teleological, or consequentialist). Starting from the foundations of his ethics, we will be able to understand Socrates' rejection of the offer to escape prison and death as both morally right *and* in his best interest.

In view of the narrowly defined scope of this study, I have concentrated on a limited number of sources, viz. only those which promised to reveal something specific about Socratic principles. Material that is intrinsically valuable but does not directly address foundational questions has not been considered. I have assumed that we have little to learn from Aristophanes and Xenophon.[1] My main sources are three early Platonic works: the *Apology*, the *Crito*, and the *Gorgias*,[2] a few passages from other dialogues; and some references to Socrates in Aristotle.[3]

Beyond the assumptions just mentioned (which are chiefly of a scholarly nature), I have also made some philosophical assumptions concerning ethics and rationality. These explain the manner in which the key questions about Socratic ethics are raised in this book.

Ethics deals with human action. In the present-day philosophical study of action, it is common to differentiate two approaches which converge at certain points but which have fundamentally different goals.

On the one hand, there is *action theory*, i.e. a discipline whose primary objective is to understand how human action works. There are boundary zones where action theory overlaps with empirical psychology and even with neurophysiology; but insofar as it analyzes the language used to express what we do in order to clarify the explanatory role of intentions and motivations, action theory should be classified as a branch of philosophy.[4]

Ethics, on the other hand, adopts an altogether different viewpoint. Its aim is not to *explain* action but to *evaluate* it; i.e., either to justify or to condemn what has been done or what we intend to do. Since we can act without any awareness of the specific explanatory function of intentions or motivations but cannot act without some sort of evaluation of what we do, ethics tends to coincide with the kind of reasoning we use when we try to decide what to do.

Action theory is a form of theoretical knowledge, whereas ethics is an instance of practical knowledge, a form of knowledge that gives direction to our own actions and those of others. In both there are abstract considerations as well as references to particular instances. It is important, therefore, not to confuse the abstract with the theoretical. There are highly abstract practical truths, and there is also theoretical consideration of particular facts. Whether one's stance is theoretical or practical at a given point depends on whether one's ultimate end is to attain truth *tout court* or truth that has action-guiding force. Needless to say, our reasoning in everyday life intertwines practical and theoretical considerations, without any special effort to sort them out.

In the study of Socratic thought, a prominent place is usually given to the problem of intellectualism. "Socratic intellectualism" is the label given to the thesis—defended by Socrates both in Plato and in Xenophon—that if a person knows an act is good for her, she will do it; if she knows it is bad, she will avoid it.[5] This is logically equivalent to the denial of *akrasia*, "incontinence," i.e., doing what one knows to be bad for oneself or failing to do what one knows to be good for oneself. Since, on occasion, we do things that are bad for us, the denial of incontinence leaves no room for the explanation of wrong choices other than ignorance on the part of the agent. The person who makes the wrong choice does so because she *does not know* that what she does is bad or what she neglects to do is good. On this view, practical failure is reduced to intellectual failure.

According to the distinction between philosophical disciplines dealing with action, Socratic intellectualism is not an ethical thesis but rather a thesis in action theory. Its aim is to *explain* the phenomenon of irrationality in action.

Explaining why apparently irrational behavior sometimes occurs is a theoretical enterprise. To determine instead which choices are indeed irrational is a practical task, since, at least initially and in an intuitive sense, we censure irrational actions and praise rational ones. This way of classifying actions implies that the adjectives involved have evaluative force.

What is meant here by "irrational" and "rational"? Underlying the whole tradition of Greek ethics is a conception of practical rationality that is formulated perhaps most clearly by Aristotle:

Every intellect [reason, *nous*] chooses what is best for itself.[6]

This implies that if an individual chooses what is not best for her, and *a fortiori* what is not even good for her, she is not making use of her rational powers. We may thus formulate a general principle of practical rationality:

(P1) A choice is rational if and only if it is a choice of what is best for the agent.

This formulation covers both choices among options that are all good and choices between what is good and what is bad. In this latter case, the choice of what is best amounts simply to the choice of the good.

This principle entails that in determining whether someone has acted rationally or not, the agent's beliefs do not count. The decisive consideration is whether what he chose to do was or was not, in fact, good (or best) for him. And this is not a subjective matter. Hence, in the light of (P1), the fundamental task of ethics consists in identifying the human goods and establishing comparisons among them. This goal of practical reasoning is often alluded to by saying that moral philosophers attempt to clarify the content of what they (in a somewhat cryptic fashion) call "the good."

The study of the history of ancient ethics shows that there was remarkable agreement on this point. All ancient moral philosophers sought to determine what the good was. They did so, for the most part, by asking, "What is *eudaimonia* (happiness, well-being, flourishing)?" i.e., what is the best possible state for humans, the state in which all (or most) goods are attained? The correct answer to this question is expected to provide the ultimate criterion for rational choice. We shall often return to this topic.

In order to gain an adequate understanding of Greek ethics, we should also note a further assumption, adopted without discussion by Aristotle and undoubtedly accepted as well by Plato and by Socrates:

(P2) For every human being, it is good to be a good human being.

A principle of this nature logically supports a formulation using superlatives:

(P2a) For every human being, the best is to be an excellent human being.

This principle, which in fact claims that the most desirable condition for a human being is to attain the highest possible quality a human being can attain—i.e., that happiness and excellence coincide—presents a fair share of difficulties. Some modern scholars believe it is false.[7] It also appears to be implicitly rejected by any ancient philosopher willing to hold that pleasure is the good. This position, commonly known as hedonism (from *hedone*, the Greek term for "pleasure"), seems to imply that pleasure makes an individual happy independent of whether or not the consistent pursuit and enjoyment of pleasure might make him a worse person, in some relevant sense of "worse." There is, of course, the option of construing (P2), or the modified version (P2a), as analytic, so that the individual devoted to the maximization of his own pleasure at all times would be, by definition, an excellent person. This is dubious, however, because the Greeks had a set of public criteria which they used to pass judgment on human excellence and its opposite. These criteria they called *aretai*, a term traditionally rendered in Latin as *virtutes* and in English as "virtues." I often use an alternative rendering, viz. "excellences," which conveys in English the conceptual connection strongly suggested by the Greek superlative of "good": whoever possesses the *aretai* is an *aristos aner*, "an excellent man."

Human excellence or, more generally, human goodness is what an individual attains when he acts in accordance with courage (ἀνδρεία), with moderation or self-control or unobtrusiveness (σωφροσύνη), with justice or honesty (δικαιοσύνη), with piety or respect for the gods (τὸ εὐσεβές, τὸ ὅσιον), with prudence or practical wisdom (σοφία, φρόνησις), etc. Within a general agreement on the basic meaning of the corresponding terms, these standards of public behavior evolved from the time of Homer through the fifth-century B.C. and beyond.[8] As Aristotle tells us, Socrates made the search for definitions of the virtues a cardinal concern of his philosophical activity.

Since Socrates may be taken to assume that practical rationality encourages an individual to seek what is best for him; and, moreover, since what is best for him is to be an excellent human being—i.e., a human being who can be commended for being courageous, moderate, just, pious, and wise[9]—we have reached by another route the initial conviction that a study of Socratic ethics should attempt to clarify the notion of human good (or happiness, i.e., the ultimate objective of our self-interest) and how it is related to the moral excellences (and to morality in general).

Does Socrates view the excellences as conducive to the good in the sense that if one practices them, they will ultimately yield, as a consequence, that desirable state called "happiness"? Or are the excellences linked to happiness in a different way, perhaps in such a way that their very practice counts as happiness? If so, are the virtues the sole ingredient of the good, or only one—perhaps the chief one—within a plurality of ingredients?

We are led to the following options:

(1) The *instrumental* interpretation of the role of the moral excellences, in which they are simply external means to achieve happiness.

(2) The *coincidental* interpretation, in which the excellences are constitutive elements of happiness. Of this there are two possible versions:

> (2a) *Complete coincidence*, if the moral excellences are the only constitutive elements of happiness, and
> (2b) *Partial coincidence*, if the moral excellences are not the only constitutive elements of happiness.[10]

Before we turn in chapters II–IV to the textual evidence that will allow us to flesh out the corresponding positions and choose among them, we must consider a serious difficulty derived from Socrates' habitual disavowal of knowledge. If we take it literally, we may have to grant that he did not develop a moral philosophy. This will be the topic of chapter I.

I

Is There a Socratic Moral Philosophy?

Socrates, as he appears in the Platonic dialogues, is a living paradox. He has become impoverished, but he nevertheless interacts with rich aristocrats such as Critias and the relatives of Plato. He implicitly criticizes Athenian democracy and yet fulfills his basic civic and military duties faithfully. He opposes an illegal measure under the democratic regime; he also disobeys orders issued by the tyrannic government of the Thirty. He is physically ugly but his beauty of soul is highly praised. He does not long for political power and yet manages to attract some of the most ambitious politicians of the day. He extols his homoerotic inclinations but refuses to engage in homosexual sex.

These apparent contradictions also extend to his philosophizing. He seems to hold that knowledge of a virtue is a necessary and sufficient condition for virtuous behavior, while denying that he has that knowledge. When he looks for the definition of a virtue, he relies on instances of that virtue which, so it seems, could only be identified by someone who already knew the definition; Socrates claims he does not know it. Moreover, we attribute to him a decisive influence on the development of Greek thought, whereas he would perhaps be ready to deny it. In fact, many people who have heard about Socrates only remember his claim to know nothing.

Hence, the first difficulty we must confront is whether it makes sense to attribute a body of moral philosophy to someone who seems flatly to deny any claim to knowledge. Is this just another aspect of the Socratic paradox, or is it an outright misinterpretation?

The difference between a contradiction and a paradox, in the sense I shall be using these terms, is that a paradox admits of resolution whereas a contradiction does not. If there is a way of showing that there is no ultimate inconsistency between Socrates the ironist and Socrates the constructive moral philosopher, the paradox will stand explained.

In what follows, I shall attempt to show that Socrates' admission of ignorance does not preclude the possibility of a substantial Socratic contribution to the field of ethics.

Let us first examine the concept of irony and the textual evidence for Socrates' disavowal of knowledge.

Three Interpretations of Disavowals of Knowledge

In several early Platonic dialogues there is a search for the definition of moral excellence. Socrates questions an interlocutor who puts forward successive replies which Socrates then rejects by way of a procedure called the *elenchus*, or "elenctic refutation." This normally consists in getting the interlocutor to accept one or more propositions which logically entail the denial of a definition he has formulated.[11] Since Socrates applies the same destructive strategy to any fresh definition submitted, and does not offer a definition of his own, the conversation ends without any accepted definition.

Socrates' method must have caused exasperation and resentment. In Book I of the *Republic*, Plato presents Thrasymachus, one of Socrates' most vigorous antagonists, who reacts in the following manner:

> (S1) Having heard this he [*SC*. Thrasymachus] gave a big sardonic laugh and said: By Heracles, this is the usual dissembling [*eironeia*] of Socrates. I knew it and had warned these people that you would not be willing to reply but would dissemble [*eironeusoio*] and would do anything rather than give an answer if someone asked you something.[12]

Thrasymachus believes that Socratic irony of the usual sort consists in the conjunction of two alleged facts: (a) that Socrates habitually refuses to give an answer and to state his own conviction with regard to the question he is putting to others, but (b) that Socrates does in fact have an answer and a conviction. Socrates is thus perceived as a dissembler, as someone who hides under a false pretense of ignorance and hence induces deceit. Irony here is the equivalent of dissimulation.

But the term "irony" (derived from its Greek counterpart εἰρωνεία) has also come to signify something rather different.[13] We say that our utterance is ironic if we use the words to mean the opposite of what they normally mean, but without intending to deceive. It would be ironic to say that the weather is fine if it is right now raining cats and dogs, or that J. S. Bach was an unimaginative composer while the Goldberg Variations are being performed. Given the appropriate context, and perhaps a certain tone of voice, no deception should occur, unless special conditions obtain.

Alcibiades alludes to this form of irony in a passage in Plato's *Symposium* where he gives an account of his past experience with Socrates:

> (S2) He listened to me, and then, most ironically [*eironikos*] and in his extremely typical and usual manner, he said: "My dear Alcibiades, I'm afraid you are not really a worthless fellow, if what you say about me happens to be true: that there is in me a power that could make you a better man. You must have seen within me an inconceivable beauty which is totally different from your good looks. If, having seen it, you are trying to strike a bargain and exchange beauty for beauty, you intend to get much more than your fair share out of me: you are trying to get true beauty in return for seeming beauty. You aim in fact to exchange 'gold for brass'."[14]

The irony that Alcibiades attributes to Socrates in this humorous passage appears at different levels. There is mocking irony in Socrates' praise of the young man ("not a worthless fellow," "not stupid," οὐ φαῦλος), because it is reasonably clear that it would be an illusion to think that he can get away with the sort of bargain he is trying to strike. But there is also irony in Socrates' concession, made in jest, that there is an inconceivable beauty within himself. If the first sort of irony could deceive someone blinded by his own self-conceit, the second one clearly would not, given what Socrates is reported to have said immediately afterward:

> (S2) But, my fortunate friend, take a closer look lest it has escaped you that I am nothing.[15]

The implication, of course, is that Socrates is far from wanting to deceive Alcibiades into thinking that he was serious in mentioning a beauty of his own far superior to Alcibiades' physical bloom. He is warning Alcibiades, precisely, *not* to take his claim seriously.

This in turn generates a third level of irony. Socrates suggests that someone who looks twice into his soul may not find anything there, a comment almost certainly interpreted as ironic by Alcibiades, who openly claims to have already seen "the statues within" Socrates' soul, which appeared to be "divine and golden, most beautiful and admirable."[16] The inner beauty is there. Socrates disavows it, but his interlocutor is not deceived.

The exchange between Alcibiades and Socrates in the *Symposium*, then, leads to a second interpretation of Socratic irony. According to the first one, (A) Socrates has knowledge, denies it, and thereby deceives people. This was Thrasymachus' view. According to the second, (B) Socrates has knowledge, denies it, but does not intend deception. It is true that some of his interlocutors may be deceived, but others will not be misled. On the other hand, it is unclear what kind of knowledge is attributed to Socrates by those who do not assume that he is dissembling.

There is a third interpretation to consider. If (A) implies lack of sincerity and (B) implies a certain form of playfulness and oftentimes mockery, nothing prevents us from assuming that perhaps Socrates is being sincere. This third interpretation may be characterized as follows: (C) Socrates denies that he has knowledge, and this may be strictly true; he is simply being honest about it.

If we were to take these three possible interpretations of Socratic irony as mutually exclusive, we would be guilty of oversimplification. It could certainly be the case that for different forms of knowledge (or for the knowledge of different sorts of items), the Socratic confession of ignorance has a different import. The correct reply, then, to the question of whether Socrates is insincere, simply playful, or straightforwardly sincere is a function of the sort of knowledge Socrates happens to be disclaiming on a given occasion.

What kinds of knowledge does Socrates disavow?

Disavowal of Knowledge in the *Apology*

The attempt to answer this important question should begin with a careful examination of the *Apology*. If this work was intended to serve as a minimally effective defense of the memory of

Socrates, we may reasonably expect it to reflect to some extent what Socrates actually said in front of the jury. Had Plato composed a speech that was radically different from the one delivered by Socrates during the actual proceedings, he would have severely weakened the case for Socrates, since many Athenians who were present at the trial would have been alive and active in politics at the time the *Apology* started to circulate.

There is a second reason to begin with the *Apology*, if indeed we can rely on its being a Platonic recreation of what went on during the trial. In it we get a picture of Socrates attempting to justify his life as a whole. Hence, his disavowal of knowledge is set in a broader context than in the early dialogues. He is trying to present his claim of ignorance as both central to his philosophical mission to Athens, and a clear indication that the accusations raised against him are false.

In fact, during the trial, Socrates had to face charges that were officially formulated in these terms:

> (S3) Socrates does wrong [ἀδικεῖ, does something unjust, commits a crime] [a] by corrupting the young and [b] by not acknowledging the gods that the city acknowledges, [c] but rather other new divinities.[17]

According to Socrates, these charges reflect "the first accusations," the charges derived from the false image of Socrates created earlier by Athenian comedians, particularly by Aristophanes. These are given a fictitious official wording by Socrates:

> (S4) Socrates does wrong [ἀδικεῖ] and busies himself [d] searching things under the earth and in the sky, and [e] making the worse argument the stronger, and [f] teaching others these same things.[18]

The direct implication of charge [d]—which represents the background for charges [b] and [c] in the official accusations—is that Socrates is a "natural philosopher"; i.e., that he belongs to that group of philosophers which Aristotle later called "the physicists" (*physikoi*).

Natural philosophy attempts to explain events in the world by recourse to the unalterable and involuntary behavior of the ultimate constituents of things. It is the innermost nature of things

and not external divine intervention that accounts for their properties and for certain occurrences.

To study "things below the earth and in the sky" (in a parallel
passage the latter are called *ta meteora*, "things aloft")[19] should be
understood as the attempt to give naturalistic explanations of geo-
logical phenomena such as earthquakes and volcanic eruptions,
on the one hand, and of meteorological phenomena (broadly conceived) such as rain, thunder or eclipses on the other. This way of
specifying the domain of natural philosophy is highly significant,
because it covers precisely the phenomena which had been traditionally taken to reveal the will of the gods. Soothsayers and
prophets who were expected to provide members of the community with religious interpretations of those events were thus likely
to regard the new physics as a threat to their craft and, if adopted
on a larger scale, as a threat to the religion of the state.[20] Socrates, as
an alleged advocate of the novel approach to nature, would, on
such a view, be guilty of atheism.

Associating Socrates with the Sophistic movement—[e],
above—would have been particularly damaging to him given the
negative sentiment toward teachers of rhetoric current at the time.
The leaders of the democratic restoration in Athens viewed the
sophists as the teachers of the young oligarchs who destroyed the
democratic constitution in 411 B.C. and who went on to participate
in the dictatorship of the Thirty after 404.[21]

Even someone like Socrates' younger friend Alcibiades, a radical democrat often suspected of aiming at tyranny, was probably
perceived as a product of the education provided by the sophists.[22]
Such utter disregard for the constitutional order is, of course, a
form of corruption, and anyone suspected of having led the young
in this direction could be labeled a corruptor of youth. We should
therefore assume a close association between charge [e] and
charges [a] and [f].[23]

It is important to observe that Socrates denies the charges and
does so by appealing to the testimony of those present at the trial.[24]
In doing so, he unmistakenly disavows knowledge within two
domains:

(1) The science of nature,[25] and

(2) the art of rhetoric, and, in general, the field of education.[26]

Since many of those attending the proceedings could bear witness to the fact that they had never heard Socrates talking about

natural philosophy, nor seen him become wealthy as a teacher of excellence, the accusers do not seem to have sufficient evidence to show the jury that Socrates was indeed a physicist and a sophist. But we do know that the accusers were politically able men who would not lightheartedly risk failure. What were they relying on when they brought forth legal action on those specific charges? What had Aristophanes had in mind many years earlier when he hoped the public would laugh if he put Socrates on stage as a representative of the new intellectuals?

We must assume, I think, that there was something about Socrates' public image that made both the caricature in the *Clouds* and the indictment effective.

According to Plato, Socrates saw the problem and faced it squarely by posing an imaginary objection:

> (S5) Perhaps one of you might retort: "But, Socrates, what is your own pursuit? Whence did these slanders arise? For surely if you had not been busying yourself with something out of the common, all this talk and gossip would not have arisen, unless you were doing something different from most people. Tell us what it is, so that we won't improvise in speaking about you." It seems to me that whoever says this is making a fair request, and I will try to show you what it is that has generated this reputation and slander.[27]

The main thrust of his reply to the hypothetical question is to connect his own pursuit with a divine source, viz. Apollo, the god of Delphi:

> (S6) Well, at one time he [= Chairephon, a friend of Socrates, now dead, who had fought for the restoration of democracy] went to Delphi and was bold enough to ask the oracle—as I said before, gentlemen, please remain silent—he asked in fact whether there was anyone wiser than I. The Pythia [= the priestess through which the god spoke and whose words were then interpreted by the priests of the sanctuary] replied that no one was wiser.[28]

Socrates' reaction to this pronouncement was marked by initial puzzlement, a natural reaction on the part of someone who is aware of his own ignorance:

> (S7) I am conscious of not being wise in anything great or small.[29]

Anyone seriously convinced of this would be naturally inclined
to think that Apollo's pronouncement must be false. It is reasonable to expect that there will be someone wiser than a person who
is not wise at all. But this, according to Socrates, is intolerable:

(S8) For he [= the god] surely does not lie; it is not right [θέμις] for
him to do so.[30]

Hence, if the statement

"Socrates is wise"

is known by Socrates himself to be false, but the god affirms something which implies that it is true (and his truthfulness cannot be
doubted), then the only way out for Socrates is to suppose that the
god is speaking in riddles, a not uncommon expectation on the
part of those consulting the oracle.[31]

Accordingly, Socrates sets out to inquire into the *meaning* of the
pronouncement, not into its *truth*.[32] And yet, at least formally, his
inquiry seems to aim at refuting the oracle by showing that the
claim that no one is wiser than Socrates is false. Socrates' inquiry
takes on the task of trying to find someone who surpasses him in
wisdom. Finding such an individual would amount to providing
a decisive counterexample to the pronouncement of the oracle.

Socrates proceeds to question individuals classified as politicians, poets and craftsmen; i.e., individuals who are expected to be
superior to him in their respective domains and who therefore
would qualify as being wiser.

Among representatives of the first group, Socrates detects the
appearance of wisdom (especially in their own eyes) but no true
knowledge. Socrates infers that he is slightly wiser than they are
because neither he nor they "know anything fine and good" [οὐδὲν
καλὸν κἀγαθόν]; but he, at least, does not think he knows what he
does not know.[33] The expression *ouden kalon kagathon*, used here
without the article, does not stand for "the fine and the good",[34]
i.e., for the primary object of moral knowledge. Rather it suggests
that what politicians claim to have, and do not, is the general kind
of evaluative knowledge needed to manage the affairs of the state
on a day-to-day basis. Socrates is not disavowing moral knowledge.

The poets, in turn, say many fine things "by some inborn nature and from inspiration" and hence, strictly speaking, "do not understand anything they say."[35] This in itself is not to be regarded as a particularly negative trait of poetry. What seems intolerable to Socrates is that

(S9) because of their poetry they thought they were the wisest of men in other subjects in which they were not [*sc.* wise].[36]

The poets, then, seem to make two different claims: to know how to compose poetry (but they actually do not *know* because they are driven by the nonrational force of inspiration) and to know about matters outside the domain of poetry (and again in this area they turn out to be ignorant).[37]

In the craftsmen, Socrates also detected a step beyond the boundaries of their fields of competence. Members of this group are here called χειροτέχναι, "handcrafters," i.e., "people who work with their hands." They include carpenters, shoemakers, builders, etc., and also those we would call sculptors, painters, architects, etc., and even physicians. Common to all of them is the fact that they generate a product or work (ἔργον, *ergon*). This product may or may not be a tangible object. A musical performer is also a craftsman of a sort, as is a doctor, though health, the goal of the doctor, is not an object in the normal sense of the word. Socrates admits that

(S10) . . . they knew things I did not know and in this respect they were wiser than I. And yet, Athenians, our good craftsmen also seemed to me to have exactly the same shortcoming as the poets: because of the fine exercise of his craft each of them claimed [ἠξίου] to be very wise also in other most important matters, and this excess of theirs overclouded the wisdom they had.[38]

The craftsmen, then, while knowledgeable (ἐπιστάμενοι, having *episteme* or "science") in their own craft (τέχνη, *techne*), are also said to claim knowledge of "the greatest things" (τὰ μέγιστα), an expression which the jurors doubtless understood as a reference to the domain of politics.[39] Within the context of the relatively small Greek city-state, the most important decisions were indeed the political ones. Frequently, not only the welfare but even the life of the citizens was a function of the wisdom of certain policies or of particular decrees. But the sharpest among the jurors must have also perceived a veiled criticism of democracy, a system that allows craftsmen to attend the meetings of the Assembly and make decisions about matters that lie beyond their field of competence. Hence, when he claims that he is "neither wise in their wisdom nor ignorant in their ignorance," Socrates is disavowing craft knowledge and political expertise.[40] He is not disavowing moral knowledge.

Note that Socrates takes craft-knowledge to be a genuine form of knowledge while denying that alleged forms of knowledge which cannot be construed as a peculiar craft or skill, such as the insight of the politician or the inspiration of the poet, have any value at all. The Socratic claim of ignorance has now been extended to three new areas:

(3) politics,

(4) poetry,

(5) craft-knowledge.

If we pause for a moment and ask how we should understand Socrates' disavowals in these areas, we will arrive at relatively unproblematic answers for items (1) natural philosophy, (4) poetry, and (5) the crafts.

In the *Phaedo* there is a well-known autobiographical passage where Socrates describes his initial interest in, and ultimate disappointment with, inquiries of the sort earlier philosophers engaged in.[41] Hence, we can readily explain the reference in the *Apology* to Anaxagoras and his doctrines,[42] but it is clear that Socrates is in no way committed to the truth of these or other explanations of natural phenomena. Socrates had long given up such pursuits, as those present could attest. Moreover, it is also reasonably clear that Socrates was neither a poet nor a craftsman.[43]

If we consider (3), i e., Socrates' claim of ignorance in political matters, a contradiction seems to arise because of Socrates' claim in the *Gorgias* that he is "the only one among [his] contemporaries who engages in politics."[44] This startling piece of self-interpretation, however, appears in a dialogue written later which develops the view that the improvement of the citizens is not a peculiar duty of a philosopher functioning in a private capacity, but a primary duty of the state as such. Hence the qualification "the true political craft" included in the wording of this alleged

Socratic claim. It is easy to see, of course, that we are here only one step away from the specifically Platonic thesis that philosophers should wield political power because they are the only ones who have adequate knowledge of the eternal and unchanging Forms.[45]

By contrast, Socrates' reluctance to participate in the deliberations of the Athenian Assembly or of the Council (though he is willing to do so when strictly required by law)—that is, his unwillingness to engage in the day-to-day managing of the state; i.e., in politics in the ordinary sense of that word[46]—is consistent with his having no special insight into the best way to conduct contingent public affairs. It is safe, therefore, to assume that Socrates is being sincere when he professes to be as ignorant as Athens' practicing politicians.

Finally, Socrates' avowal of ignorance with regard to (2), the teaching of rhetoric, leads him to deny that he attempts to educate young men. To be able to educate in the sense in which the sophists profess to educate, one would have to have knowledge of "political" excellence, i.e., of the excellence that makes for successful politicians.[47] There is, therefore, a close connection between disavowing knowledge in domain (2), the specific area of sophistic expertise, and in (3), the alleged area of competence of Athens' practicing politicians. We must emphasize once more that when Socrates disavows knowledge in areas in which sophists and politicians claim it, he is not claiming moral ignorance.

If these reflections are correct, Socrates' disavowal of knowledge in areas (1) through (5) can be interpreted as instances of (C): Socrates is simply being honest in admitting his lack of expertise in fields in which he genuinely has none.

Another, rather specific instance of the Socratic avowal of ignorance must be examined. Given the penalty assessed by his accusers, Socrates is confronted with the prospect of death. In reply to a new hypothetical objection that fear of death should have made him feel ashamed of his "occupation," he says:

(S11) . . . to fear death, gentlemen, is nothing but to think that one is wise when one is not, for it is to think that one knows what one doesn't know. No one, in fact, knows death nor whether it happens to be the greatest of all goods for a man, and yet people are afraid of it as if they knew very well that it was the greatest of evils. And isn't this the most blameworthy ignorance, to think one knows what one doesn't know? By this much and in this respect too, gentlemen, I am perhaps different from most people; and if I were to say that I am wiser than someone in some respect, it would be in this: that having no adequate knowledge about things in Hades [= the underworld, the realm of the dead], I likewise do not think I have it.[48]

We must therefore add to our list of those things encompassed by the Socratic disavowal of knowledge the following:
(6) death.
What Socrates claims not to know about death is not so much what kind of event it is, but rather what its correct evaluation should be: whether it is the best thing that can happen to someone or the worst thing. In his denial of possessing this evaluative knowledge, Socrates is not being insincere or ironic. His disavowal is, again, of type (C): he denies knowing something which could only be accessible to someone who has experienced the state that follows death. Neither he nor anyone else, of course, knows what that state is like.[49]
If we look at the early dialogues which have at their center the search for the definition of a moral excellence, we find one more item to add to the list of things Socrates claims not to know:
(7) the excellences or virtues, virtue in general, and their respective definitions.
The inclusion of this class of objects among the things Socrates claims not to know generates a difficulty that did not arise with the previous items on our list. We here seem to be confronted with a specific disavowal of moral knowledge.
Before facing this new difficulty, it is important to call attention to the fact that there are numerous passages in which Socrates affirms that he *does* know something. Socratic irony is not equivalent to a form of radical skepticism.

Socratic Claims to Knowledge

Some Socratic claims to knowledge are based on everyday experience and commonsense reflection on it:

(S12) And yet I know [οἶδα] well enough that these words make me unpopular, which also proves that I am telling the truth.[50]
(S13) For I know very well [εὖ γὰρ οἶδα] that wherever I go and speak, the young will listen to me as they do here.[51]

We should also recall those passages in which the object of knowledge is immediately present to Socrates' consciousness:

(S14) = (S7) I am conscious [σύνοιδα ἐμαυτῷ] of not being wise in anything great or small.[52]

(S15) For I was conscious [ἐμαυτῷ γὰρ συνῄδη] of knowing nothing, so to speak.[53]

Of greater interest for the present inquiry are the lines that immediately follow (S15), the statement of uncertainty about the evaluation of death:

(S16) That to do what's unjust and to disobey one's superior, be he god or man, is bad [κακόν] and shameful [αἰσχρόν], that I do know [οἶδα; the position of the verb is emphatic]. Hence, I shall never fear or flee from things of which I do not know whether they even happen to be good [in this case, death] instead of from bad things which I know to be bad [in this case, injustice and disobedience].[54]

In this passage, the only one of its kind in the early dialogues, Socrates declares that he possesses evaluative knowledge of two types of acts: acts of injustice and acts of disobedience. He claims to know (i) that each of them is shameful (αἰσχρόν). The Greek predicate makes clear in this instance that the evaluation is moral. To say that what someone has done is *aischron* is to label it as ugly and dishonorable, as blameworthy from the moral point of view. But Socrates also claims to know (ii) that each of them is bad (κακόν).

Since *kakon* in Greek (and "bad" in English) can be used in both a moral and a nonmoral sense, it is not clear how we should understand Socrates' second claim. An action such as lying to a friend can be said to be bad because it is blameworthy, but something can also be bad without moral implications, such as being mistaken. We are worse off if we make a mistake about a certain state of affairs than we would be if we had got it right, but being mistaken does not make us wicked.

The subsequent contrast, however, between things known to be bad, and death, which may turn out to be good, strongly suggests that the occurrence of "bad" here is an instance of the nonmoral use. The goodness or badness of death can only be the nonmoral quality of that mysterious event.[55] We shall return to this point shortly.

Setting aside disobedience as a particular case of injustice, we can recapitulate Socrates' claim in (S16) as follows:

> (a) I know that injustice is shameful and bad.

We can readily assume that this statement implies a symmetrical statement:

> (b) I know that justice is fine and good.[56]

An Avowal of Moral Ignorance

Let us note that Book I of the *Republic* ends with the following words:

> (S17) For, so long as I do not know what the just [= justice] is, I will hardly know whether it happens to be an excellence or not, and whether he who possesses it is unhappy or happy.[57]

In this context, to say that something designated by the neuter adjective or the abstract noun is an excellence (*arete*, "virtue") implies that the corresponding predicate can be used to commend someone from the moral point of view. If justice is a virtue, then to say that someone is just is to morally praise him for that noble and praiseworthy attribute. On the other hand, "to be happy" is first and foremost a nonmoral attribute, since happiness (εὐδαιμονία, flourishing) is understood as the possession of an abundance of those things which make us better off, and normally people take these to be the nonmoral goods.[58] Hence, *mutatis mutandis* it is fair to say that (S17) entails that Socrates is claiming:

> (c) I do not know whether justice is fine and good.

It seems obvious that (b) and (c) are contradictory statements.

If we accepted (c) as a genuine Socratic belief and rejected (b), we would have to admit that there is no Socratic moral philosophy, since it is natural to assume that a system of philosophical ethics would include evaluations such as the one expressed by the subordinate clause of (c). Socrates, however, claims not to know whether it is true or false.

In order to show that the conjunction of (b) and (c) does not constitute a contradiction but rather a paradox, it is useful to ask how an Athenian would have reacted to someone's claim not to know whether justice is or is not an *arete*, i.e., a noble and praiseworthy quality.

The early dialogues provide us with an interesting clue. On two similar occasions, Socrates asks an interlocutor whether courage and self-control, respectively, are among the (very, πάνυ) fine (admirable, noble) things. In each case, not only does the person respond with great, positive assurance, but in one instance he even adds an emphatic comment on Socrates' conviction regarding such clear matters: "You really know well that it is one of the noblest."[59]

Since, like "courageous" and "self-controlled," the predicate equivalent to "just" was used in ordinary Greek for moral commendation,[60] Socrates' claim not to know whether justice is an excellence can hardly have been taken seriously by his audience, because doubting such an obvious truth was an oddity. Its truth is pellucid because of the very meaning of the terms "justice" and "virtue." Hence, they probably understood him as expressing irony of type (B), i.e., possessing the knowledge he disclaimed, but playfully denying it.

Socrates' plea of ignorance as to whether or not justice produces happiness is not as simple to interpret. As I shall try to show in chapter III, it is a substantive moral question and not a self-evident truth readily available to members of the community by virtue of the language they speak.

At the end of *Republic* Book I the connections between happiness and justice are not clarified because no satisfactory definition of the latter is found. This failure is realized in the midst of an impassioned and at times tense conversation. Yet the discussion itself was a free and open-ended exchange, proceeding with no urgency to make any specific, practical decision. A practical notion is subject to scrutiny, but the dramatic setting makes it clear that the connection with actual choice and action is remote. Socrates has gone down to the Piraeus to attend a religious festival and is invited to the house of Cephalus. Upon hearing the host's reflections on the prospect of dying while still owing sacrifices to a god, or money to a man—i.e., having failed to redress instances of injustice—Socrates takes the occasion to ask, in general, what justice is. There is, however, no urgency to resolve any particular instance of injustice.

Strictly speaking, Socrates' final admission of ignorance in Book I of the *Republic*, whether or not it is good to fulfill the requirements of justice, would, if in earnest, cast him as someone who has drastically abandoned any sensible rule for morally correct action. "Just" can be taken in many contexts as a predicate that characterizes all action that is morally right and praiseworthy. "Good," in turn, stands for an attribute that provides the ultimate reason for doing something. Hence, it is doubtful that Socrates' friends would have been led to think that he had adopted a radical moral agnosticism that would have left him without any rational justification to behave in a morally upright manner. It seems more likely that this part of his closing remarks should also be understood as ironic in sense (B), i.e., as implying the contrary of what he said, without thereby intending to deceive.

If these conjectures are correct, we must hold that Socrates does indeed know that justice is praiseworthy and worth having; i.e., that it is something fine and good, as stated in (b). But how are we to explain his denial in *Republic* I, and his affirmation in the *Apology*, of those very same convictions?

The trial, of course, is not by any means the appropriate setting for what I have called a "free and open-ended discussion." The way Socrates chooses to conduct his defense makes it even more removed from a free form of exchange. Socrates describes his predicament as his being forced to choose between obeying Apollo, even at the risk of his own life, and preserving his life at the cost of disobeying the divine injunction. In the face of such a dramatic choice, Socrates declares that choosing the second option follows from the belief that one knows that death is something bad, whereas choosing the first option is a consequence of believing that disobedience and injustice are bad. Socrates asserts that he does not know whether the former of these two beliefs is true or not, but he does claim to know that the latter is true. *The inescapable need to choose between life and death (and to justify his choice) leads Socrates openly and firmly to avow, at least once, that he knows something of considerable moral import.*

I have argued that Socrates' sincere disavowals of knowledge in politics, poetry, and the crafts do not imply sincere disavowals of moral knowledge. The domain, beyond their skills, to which the craftsmen extended their claims—and within which Socrates also declared himself incompetent—was the domain of contingent political matters, not the field of moral philosophy.

In contrast, as I mentioned above, Socrates does disavow moral knowledge in some of the early aporetic dialogues. However, those denials should not be understood either as sincere or as insincere and hence as misleading disavowals. But if Socrates is not being insincere, why does he not abandon the ironic stance and declare that he knows what the corresponding moral excellence is?

A brief examination of some aspects of the *Euthyphro* may be helpful at this point.

Euthyphro's Claim to Knowledge

During a conversation with Socrates at the Portico of the Archon-King in the Athenian *agora*, Euthyphro declares that he is prosecuting his father for murder in a rather obscure case involving the death of a laborer who had killed a slave and who was neglected while the father awaited official instructions as to what he should do with the man. Since the popular notion of piety involves respect for the gods and for one's parents, Euthyphro seems to be doing something which most men would hesitate to do. Most men would not seek punishment for their fathers because they would not know whether they were doing the right thing or not.[61] Hence Socrates' question:

(S18) Soc.: By Zeus, Euthyphro, do you think your knowledge of divine matters, and of pious and impious things, is so accurate [ἀκριβῶς] that even if things happened as you say, you are not afraid of doing something impious yourself in prosecuting your father?

Euth.: I would be worthless, Socrates, and Euthyphro would be no different from the common run of men, if I did not know all such things accurately [ἀκριβῶς].[62]

Here the emphasis clearly falls on the self-assurance with which Euthyphro claims to have strict knowledge (the opposite would be to know τύπῳ, "roughly," "in broad outline")[63] about things divine and the right and wrong ways to relate to them. Only some-

one who has such exact knowledge would run the moral risk
Euthyphro is assuming by taking his father to court. A very fine
line separates Euthyphro's action, if it is indeed a requirement of
piety to prosecute a wrongdoer even if it is your father,[64] from an
impious undertaking.

As the dialogue proceeds, Socrates offers his assessment of the
kind of precise knowledge that the circumstances require: one
would have to know the character or trait (ἰδέα, εἶδος, "aspect,"
"form") that is common to all pious actions and in virtue of which
they are pious.[65] Once that is identified, one should look upon it
and use it as a model or standard (παράδειγμα, "paradigm") to
decide whether a particular event is or is not an instance of piety.[66]
It is a further Socratic assumption that the definition of a moral
term is expected to capture such a character or trait.

In the remainder of the dialogue, Socrates' strategy consists in
an attempt to undermine Euthyphro's self-assurance by showing
him that he does not know how to define piety. Every definition
proposed or accepted by Euthyphro is rejected once it is subjected
to a Socratic counterargument. The outcome is that Euthyphro is
shown not to have a clear view of the standard that would allow
him to judge with confidence whether or not he is doing the right
thing.

If we reflect on the whole dialogue, we will feel compelled to
say that any witness to the conversation (or a modern reader, for
that matter) would walk away convinced that Socrates' requests
to become Euthyphro's pupil, because of the former's own ignorance in divine affairs, are made in jest.[67] The firm direction in
which he guides the conversation suggests that Socrates is by no
means in the dark with regard to the topic under scrutiny. It is
Socrates who introduces the notion of establishing justice as the
generic concept under which piety may be subsumed,[68] and it is
also under his initiative that "service [or the art of serving,
ὑπηρετική] to the gods" is substituted for the misleading expression "care [θεραπεία] of the gods."[69] The latter suggests, inappro-
priately (like "therapy," the English term derived from it), that the
object of our care may be improved. The former is an expression
which Socrates can earnestly apply to his own obedience to the
oracle: "I believe no greater good has come to you in the city than
this service of mine to the god."[70] Finally, Socrates does not hesitate to indicate in the *Euthyphro* that he does have views about the

gods: he finds stories about immoral behavior on their part hard to accept. In the *Apology*, we saw this conviction surface as one of the key assumptions in his interpretation of the oracle given to Chairephon: Apollo, the god of Delphi, cannot lie.

Euthyphro's initial claim can be accounted for as follows:

When an individual claims to know, (i) he states that he has true beliefs within a given domain, and (ii) he is confident that his beliefs are unshakably true and, hence, not open to revision.

Ignorance on the part of an individual who claims to know will then obtain if his beliefs are false and therefore his confidence turns out to be unfounded.

Socratic Wisdom

In light of the proposed analysis of Euthyphro's claim, we can understand Socrates' disavowal of knowledge as a denial that he has true beliefs or as a denial that his beliefs are definitely settled.

As we have seen, Socrates does admit lack of true beliefs in certain domains: cases (1) through (6), i.e., in physics, rhetoric, politics, poetry, the crafts, and death.

With respect to his denial of knowledge of items in (7), viz. the moral virtues, it seems reasonable to assume that Socrates recognizes that he does not totally lack true opinions or convictions (otherwise, as we saw, he would be a man without a moral rudder, something hard to extract from our sources). In all likelihood he wishes to deny that he has firm and unshakable knowledge of the moral virtues, and thus that he remains open to a reexamination of his beliefs.

With regard to many of Socrates' convictions, such scrutiny has often taken place, but this does not lead him to give up, in principle, the possibility of further revision of his views, as is suggested by the wording of the following passage from the *Crito*:

(S19) Soc.: But, my admirable friend, this argument [λόγος] we have gone through still seems to me to be the same as it did before. Examine in turn the following one [to see] if it still holds good for us or not, namely that it is not to live that should be deemed most important, but to live well.

Crito: It holds good.
Soc.: And that to live well and finely and justly are the same, does
this hold good or does it not hold good?
Crito: It does hold good.[71]

The repeated expression "hold good" translates a Greek word
(μένει) which conveys the idea of something remaining as it was,
standing fast even though it could have changed or given way.
This suggests that the two friends have agreed in the past on the
truth of the statements, and that Socrates wants to know whether
Crito still abides by these convictions or has had reason to change
his mind about them. The possibility of reopening the discussion
is not precluded in principle, but in this circumstance they move
on.[72]

In the privacy of his cell, Socrates can remind Crito of past conversations and resulting agreements. He can gently inquire
whether Crito wants to revise them or not. This he cannot do in the
confrontation with his judges. Hence the dogmatic tone Socrates
employs in (S16) where, without hesitation, he claims to know that
something is true: that injustice and disobedience are bad and
shameful. His confidence, we may suppose, is derived from the
fact that he has often considered the point and found no reason to
believe it false. It is conceivable that in a different setting Socrates
might have been willing to reopen a discussion of even this fundamental piece of moral knowledge.

In the context of the *Apology* and the *Crito*, we find no indication
of what would count as settled true belief, and therefore of what
would constitute stable, definitive knowledge.[73] We are offered
instead two passages that may confirm the suggestion that in those
cases where Socratic irony seems to be insincere, it amounts, in
fact, to Socrates' willingness to revise his own moral convictions:

(S20) For I, gentlemen of Athens, have acquired this reputation from
nothing but a certain wisdom. What sort of wisdom is this? The one
which is perhaps human wisdom, for in fact it may be I am wise in
this sense. Those men, the ones I just mentioned [= the sophists], are
perhaps wise in a wisdom more than human. Otherwise I do not
know what to call it, for I in fact do not possess it. Whoever says I do
is lying and speaks to slander me.[74]

And further on:

(S21) I'm afraid, gentlemen, that in fact the god [= Apollo] is wise and that by means of the oracle he is saying that human wisdom is worth little or nothing. He seems to mention this man Socrates, using my name and proposing me as an example, as if he said: "He is the wisest among you, who, like Socrates, recognizes that he is truly worth nothing with respect to wisdom."[75]

Socrates' suggestion in (S20) that there is a form of sophistic wisdom that is more than human is certainly ironic. We are not deceived. The distinction that these passages make is a distinction between the divine wisdom of Apollo and the human wisdom of Socrates. It is not a bold guess that the former fully satisfies the conditions that make the claim to knowledge definitive: divine wisdom embraces true beliefs and the unshakable conviction that they are indeed true. Socratic wisdom, on the other hand, is either a sincere admission of not possessing true beliefs about certain matters, or an openness to the reexamination of beliefs previously accepted as true.

If this is correct, we have failed to discover any instance of insincere Socratic disavowals of knowledge. To do so would require identifying matters which Socrates, in principle, refuses to submit to reexamination, and of which he also denies knowledge. Thrasymachus' accusations, we can now affirm, amount to a deep misunderstanding of the fundamental Socratic attitude toward knowledge.

The alleged contradiction that arises when Apollo affirms, and Socrates denies, the assertion

Socrates is wise

has now been resolved by reinterpreting the predicate.

At the outset, Socrates takes the word "wise" to mean "a person who knows and who is justifiably confident that he does indeed know." After his search for someone wiser than he, Socrates realizes that what Apollo meant was "a person who makes no claim to know with full confidence."

If this is correct, the path of inquiry into Socratic ethics has cleared a major obstacle. Socrates' disavowal of moral knowledge should not be taken to imply Socrates' strict lack of knowledge, but rather his consistent willingness to reexamine his convictions.

This suggests that Socrates views his moral philosophy not as divine wisdom, i.e., as a definitive and unshakable system, but rather as a body of ideas he is willing to modify or even to abandon, should he be offered persuasive objections.

We may conclude, then, that there is no ultimate inconsistency between Socrates the ironist and Socrates the constructive moral philosopher.

II

Fundamentals of Ethics in the *Apology*

In the *Apology*, as I have suggested, Socrates asserts that he knows that injustice and disobedience are shameful and bad because he needs to justify a decision. In this chapter we shall try to take a closer look at that decision in order to discover the general conception of ethics underlying the arguments offered by Socrates in his own defense.

Socrates has been accused of committing an injustice (ἀδικεῖν), a legal charge which carries with it moral opprobrium. One of the specific charges, that of corrupting the young, makes this sufficiently clear. The same thing could be said of the accusation that Socrates does not honor the gods honored by the city: there appears to be both a legal and a moral obligation to uphold such religious duties, probably in the sense that they were an important subset of the moral obligations of every citizen.[76]

In his defense, Socrates does not challenge the law under which the kinds of actions he is accused of performing are crimes or moral trespasses. His line of defense is to argue that he has not engaged in such activities.[77]

Socrates' life's work, which makes him the target of generalized mistrust and hatred, is quite different. In many cases, it results in his exposing to public scrutiny the false wisdom of prominent individuals and subjecting himself to retaliation. Hence the question arises as to whether or not an activity of this nature, i.e., one which may have dire consequences for the practitioner, is a blameworthy activity, an activity from which one should refrain for moral reasons.

In the *Apology* this question appears in the guise of a hypothetical objection entertained by Socrates as in (S5) when he tries to explain why his accusers, as well as the earlier comedians, were confident that the public would identify him as a physicist or a sophist.

The new objection and Socrates' reply provide an important insight into his ethics:

> (S22) Perhaps someone might say: "Aren't you ashamed [οὐκ αἰσχύνῃ, an expression of moral reproach], Socrates, to have practiced an occupation such that because of it you now face the danger of dying?" To him I would give a fair explanation in reply [δίκαιον λόγον ἀντείποιμι]: "You are wrong, my friend, if you think that a man who is worth anything should take into account the risk of living or dying instead of considering only this when he performs an action: whether his actions are just or unjust, [i.e.] the deeds of good man or of a bad one."[78]

What follows in the text is the example of Achilles, the hero who killed Hector and thus fulfilled his duty of avenging his friend Patroclus, knowing full well that his action would result in his own death shortly thereafter. The passage then continues:

> (S22 cont.) Do you think he [= Achilles] took death and danger into account? For the truth of the matter, gentlemen, is as follows: wherever someone has positioned himself [ἑαυτὸν τάξῃ] in the belief that it is for the best, or has been placed [ταχθῇ] by his commander, there, it seems to me, he should remain and face danger, and in no way take into account [the risk of] death nor anything else, instead of the shameful [πρὸ τοῦ αἰσχροῦ, in preference to the consideration of what is morally blameworthy].[79]

The hypothetical objection arises out of one of the strands of heroic ethics, the ethics that determines the code of conduct which the Homeric chieftains adhere to. Within that code, the good or excellent man is the man who prevails in individual combat and whose prowess is recognized by his peers in the form of *time* or honor.

Within that ancient value system, the *arete* of a man coincides with his ability to succeed in combat. Lack of excellence, that is, badness (in this peculiar sense of the term), is coextensive with the sort of inability which leads to defeat. To be *kakos*, "bad," is to be physically weak, ineffective, wanting in manhood (*anandros*), and incapable of defending oneself from insult and aggression. In sum, to be *kakos* is to fail as a warrior. This kind of badness is despicable and shameful, even though it may be involuntary.

Therefore, the objection faced by Socrates has the following ring to it: 'Aren't you ashamed of having run the risk of failure, since the consequence of your occupation could be the ultimate form of failure, namely, death?'

Anyone familiar with the heroic outlook will be struck by the peculiar force of the objection. Hence, the deliberate appeal to the example of Achilles, the Homeric hero *par excellence*, in Socrates' reply. But the reference to the son of Thetis is employed by Socrates to emphasize a different strand of heroic ethics, the strand within which honor can prevail to the extreme of requiring the hero to give up his own life for honor's sake. In fact, had Achilles refused to avenge Paroclus, his *time* would have been seriously affected. He would have been considered a worthless, despicable fellow. And this, for him, would have been worse than death.

In (S22) Socrates formulates a principle which in his opinion governs Achilles' decision, but which in fact also represents a revolution against the heroic outlook by placing justice above excellence in combat (and the honor which constitutes its reward). It could be reformulated as follows:

(P3) Every agent, in performing an action, should consider *exclusively* whether what he is about to do is just or unjust.

This principle is meant to preclude consideration of the non-moral consequences of an action. Whether one might suffer considerable harm, even the loss of life or reputation, should not be a consideration in reaching a decision. The principle exclusively invokes the moral attributes of an action.

In (S22) there is also a more particular version of principle (P3) which evokes a post-Homeric military context. The chief agent is no longer restricted to the hero who, like Achilles or Hector, stands on his chariot with his charioteer beside him, and then dismounts to manifest his excellence in singular combat; it is now the mass of the citizens fighting on foot and shoulder to shoulder. If we look at the two scenarios separately, we get:

(P4) Every agent who has taken a position in the belief that it is for the best ought to remain in his post.
(P5) Every agent whose post has been assigned to him by his commanding officer ought to remain in his post.

A violation of (P5) and, perhaps to a lesser degree, (P4) would imply choosing the avoidance of wounds or of death in preference to avoiding what is *aischron*, morally blameworthy.

The version most acceptable to the judges is clearly (P5), and it is therefore understandable that Socrates would invoke it to encourage the acceptance of (P3), the more general version of the same idea. In fact, (P5) expresses a requirement essential to the tactics of heavy infantry combat, a form of combat with which every Athenian citizen was familiar. The commander assigns a post in the ranks (*taxeis*) to every soldier or hoplite where he is expected to lock shields with the man on his left and the man on his right, letting his spear emerge on the right. In this manner, the ranks of hoplites appear to the enemy as a solid wall bristling with lances. If, in fear, a soldier abandons his post in the front ranks (the standard expression for this in Greek is *lipein ten taxin*), an opening is created which offers the enemy an excellent opportunity to penetrate the otherwise impregnable formation. At this moment the chief advantage of hoplite tactics is lost and defeat may readily ensue.

In this context, (P5) turns out to be obviously true for any Athenian. Socrates bears witness to the fact that he has observed it on at least three occasions. Now he regards it as applicable to different circumstances:

> (S23) [immediately following (S22)] For I would have done something dreadful, gentlemen, if, when placed [*ettaton*] by the commanders you elected to command me at Potidaea, Amphipolis and Delium, I had remained where they placed [*ettaton*] me and risked death like anybody else and then, when the god [= Apollo] commanded [*tattontos*], as I thought and understood, that I ought to live philosophizing and examining myself and others, I had abandoned the ranks [*lipoimi ten taxin*] out of fear of death or something else. That would have been dreadful . . .[80]

As we can see, Socrates regards his philosophical vocation, his call to annoy his fellow citizens with his questions, as the assignment of a post in the ranks by a superior. Here, the commanding officer is Apollo and the assignment of a position constitutes a divine mission.

What would correspond, in this case, to abandonment of the

ranks? Once more, Socrates envisages hypothetical circumstances in which this could occur:

> (S24) So that, even if you release me . . . if furthermore you said to me: "Socrates, we shall not be persuaded by Anytus [= the chief accuser]. We shall release you but on this condition: that you no longer practice this kind of inquiry and stop philosophizing; and, if you are caught still doing this, you shall die." If, as I said, you would release me on such conditions, I would reply to you: "I have regard and affection for you, gentlemen, but I will obey the god rather than you, and as long as I breathe and am able to do so, I shall not cease to philosophize. . . . "[81]

Socrates conceives his predicament as a dilemma. His marching orders would be clearly contradictory:

the god commands that I philosophize,

whereas

the Athenians command that I not philosophize,

as a condition for my being released and spared from execution.

An irreconcilable conflict arises in the application of (P5), for the assignment of two different and mutually exclusive posts is implied. Socrates resolves the issue by choosing to obey the higher authority—in this case, Apollo. Under Apollo's orders, to stop philosophizing is, for Socrates, equivalent to abandoning his assigned post.

A Divine Command Theory?

Let us consider here the structure of the ethical system which underlies the principles and particular instances that we have discovered in the *Apology*. The emphasis placed on the response of the Delphic oracle, and its interpretation on the part of Socrates, may lead us to conclude that *Socratic ethics has as its ultimate foundation a divine command*. An ethical conception along these lines justifies or condemns on the basis of dictates stemming from a god who commands, allows, or prohibits certain kinds of action. No further reason can be, or need be, invoked beyond the divine injunction. The cornerstone for this conception of ethics is the divine will.

It is indeed true that in order to counter the charge of impiety, Socrates' defense tends to highlight his obedience to what he conceives as a mission imposed upon him by Apollo, a god in whom the Athenians believe. But it would be wrong to think this constitutes the ultimate foundation of his ethics.

Notice that, in (S20), disobedience "to one's superior, be he god or man," seems to be a particular instance of a more general notion, the notion of *adikein*, "to commit a crime," "to commit an injustice," "to do what's wrong or illicit." Hence, actions performed in obedience to divine commands would only be a subset of the morally correct or right actions.

Socrates' conviction (S8) that—contrary to Homeric mythology—Apollo is precluded from lying because there is a universal order (*themis*) which he cannot transgress indicates Socrates' belief in a norm that is higher than the divine will. The ultimate foundation of ethics is not what a god chooses to command, but rather an objective order which binds even the divine will.

Furthermore, the Socratic conviction that the gods are subject to higher forms of normativity is explicitly developed in the *Euthyphro*. In fact, this conviction contributes to the plausibility of the charge of impiety against Socrates because it implies a drastic revision of popular beliefs about the behavior of the gods. The following is the relevant passage:

(S25) Euth.: [. . .] For these very same people happen to believe that Zeus is the best and most just of the gods, and at the same time agree that he bound his own father [= Cronus] because he [= Cronus] swallowed his sons contrary to what is right, and that he [= Cronus] in turn castrated *his* father [= Uranus, the Sky] on similar grounds.[. . .]
Soc.: Isn't it because of this, Euthyphro, that I'm being accused? For when someone says such things about the gods, I have trouble accepting them.[. . .] But, tell me, by the god of friendship, do you truly believe that's how it happened?
Euth.: Yes, and still more amazing things have happened, Socrates, that the majority don't know about.
Soc.: Hence, you also believe there is really a war among the gods themselves, and terrible quarrels and battles and other such things told by the poets and with which our temples are adorned by our

good friends the painters? Indeed, in the Great Panathenaea, the
robe of the goddess [= Athena] which is carried up to the Acropolis
is full of such embroideries. Shall we say that all of that is true,
Euthyphro?

Euth.: Not only that, Socrates. As I just said, I can tell you, if you
wish, many other things about the gods that I know will surprise
you when you hear them.

Soc.: I would not be surprised.[82]

The sharp contrast between what Euthyphro believes and what
Socrates disbelieves about the gods could not be more explicit.
Socrates refuses to accept that the gods should behave in the manner described by Euthyphro and the early Greek tradition, i.e.,
habitually and willfully violating basic moral norms. Socrates' re-
fusal implies that, in his judgment, the fact that a god might perform an action is insufficient to justify that kind of action. The
gods, in his opinion, behave differently because they always and
invariably follow a higher standard which holds both for them
and for mortal men.

The subordination of the gods to a higher standard can be seen
even more clearly in another passage from the *Euthyphro* where a
difficulty with regard to a divine command theory is raised independently of the limitations imposed by the imperfections of the
Homeric gods.

In the course of successive attempts to define piety, the attribute
of all actions which conform to the right relationship with the divine, Euthyphro proposes that the pious be defined as that which
is pleasing to the gods. The difficulty is raised that the gods are not
unanimous with regard to what pleases them, and the definition is
amended to include the notion of unanimity. The pious is now
held to be what is dear to *all* the gods.[83]

At this point, Socrates asks: "Is it the case that the pious is loved
by the gods because it is pious or is it pious because it is loved [by
them]?"[84]

The question suggests two possible interpretations of the attribution of piety to a given act:

(a) the act is pious, and *because of that* (all) the gods love it, or

(b) the act is pious *because* (all) the gods love it.

According to (b), love or approval on the part of the gods makes
the act pious. On this view, the act in and of itself is neutral. Its

moral attribute is explained by the fact that the gods enjoy it, are pleased with it, and approve of it. More generally, this implies that moral rectitude is a function of the divine will, and that the divine will, in turn, is not limited by any intrinsic feature of the act itself. To comply with fair agreements and to build temples are habits of justice and piety, repectively, because they please the gods. Homicide and an attack on one's father are unjust and impious actions because the gods happen to dislike them. But, in principle, the gods could be pleased by such actions.

In (a) the relation is reversed. The pleasure that the gods take in a particular act is not unfounded or arbitrary. There is something about the act itself that explains why the gods love it and find it pleasing. If this interpretation is correct, and if we generalize it, we arrive at the view that moral rectitude does not attach to actions from the outside. Rather it is an intrinsic attribute which actions possess *independent* of the reaction they provoke in the gods.

During the discussion, Socrates gets Euthyphro to agree that certain actions are loved by the gods because they are pious.[85] But if "pious" *means* "loved by the gods," then, substituting one term for the other, we obtain the absurdity that the gods love certain actions because they love them.[86] This disposes of interpretation (b). From this it follows that the proposed definition of piety must be incorrect because it does not reveal what piety *is*, but only what *happens* to it; i.e., that the gods are pleased with those actions which possess it. In Greek, the contrast is drawn by two terms that later became part of the quasi-technical vocabulary of philosophy: *ousia* and *pathos*, the being or essence of a thing, as opposed to what a thing happens to undergo.[87]

These considerations suggest that since (a) and (b) are mutually exclusive alternatives, Socrates favors the view that piety is an objective standard. Hence, a divine command should be obeyed not because it is divine, but rather because it commands that which is intrinsically right.

We must therefore abandon the idea that the first principle of Socratic ethics is the obligation to obey the injunctions issued by the gods. But Socrates' acceptance of normative standards which are higher than the divine will, hence absolute and unconditional, may lead us to suppose that Socratic ethics is an instance of what we call a *deontological* system of ethics.

A Deontological Theory?

The term "deontological" (derived from the Greek participle *to deon*, "that which must be done," "that which it is a duty to do") is commonly used to designate those systems of ethics which make duty the cornerstone that supports the entire building. Here, the ultimate reason to do something, the ultimate justification of an action, is the conviction that it is a duty. The consequences of the action, be they good or bad, are strictly irrelevant.

If we identify duty as the requirement prescribed by each of the excellences; e.g., if we understand justice or piety to be a standard which determines the duties we have to other human beings or to the gods, then it seems that the deontological interpretation of Socratic ethics is clearly correct.

This appears to be what (P3) expresses by emphasizing that the only relevant feature of an action is whether it is morally right or morally wrong; i.e., whether we have a duty to do it or to refrain from doing it. The central problem for deontological systems of ethics is to formulate criteria which determine when something is a duty and when it is not. This seems to explain why Socrates attached great importance to the search for definitions of the excellences. He expected correct definitions to yield such criteria.[88]

It cannot be seriously doubted that the excellences determine duties, but within Socrates' thought, as we shall see, the notion of the good plays a fundamental role. Deontological systems, however, place the good in a subordinate role. For the sake of conceptual clarity, it is useful to contrast the deontological approach with its best known alternative, the teleological one (from *telos*, the Greek word for "end," "goal"). These two options can be characterized roughly as follows:

A *deontological* system of ethics requires that the right be done regardless of the good (or evil) to which it is conducive.

A *teleological* system of ethics requires that the right be done because it is conducive to the good.[89]

In the remainder of this chapter I shall look at the scant references to the Socratic theory of the good in the *Apology*. My aim is to prepare the way for the thesis that Socratic ethics, contrary to our first impression, is not deontological, a view that will emerge more clearly toward the end of the next chapter.

My overall intention, however, is to prove that Socratic ethics is not teleological either. Like so much in our portrait of Socrates, this is a paradox; but this particular paradox, I believe, can be resolved by showing that the distinction between deontological and teleological ethics is only a frame of reference, useful for providing direction to our inquiry. In the long run, as we shall see, this distinction turns out to be inadequate for the classification of Socratic ethics.

Socratic Goods in the *Apology*

Socrates, as we saw, is standing at a hypothetical crossroads. His options are (i) to obey the Athenians, cease to philosophize, and live; or (ii) to obey the god Apollo, continue to philosophize, and die.

Socrates chooses the second alternative. A powerful reason in favor of the first one is obviously the avoidance of death. But to choose it would mean disobeying Apollo. This is the dilemma (S11) and (S16) refer to, highlighting the sharp distinction between wisdom and ignorance: choosing to avoid death entails the certainty that death is bad, whereas choosing to avoid disobedience entails the certainty that failure to obey is bad. Recall that Socrates claims he is only sure that disobedience is bad. He claims not to know whether or not death is really bad.

If the contrast is to be persuasive, the predicate "bad" must be used in the same sense in the formulation of the two options. Since, when applied to death, "bad" is to be understood in its nonmoral sense, it follows that when it qualifies disobedience and injustice, it is also being used in this sense. Hence, it is fair to say, Socrates is convinced that disobedience and injustice are not only morally shameful, but also bad; i e., they are things that harm us, just as an accident or sickness would harm us.

It follows that Socrates would have not only a moral reason to avoid disobedience but also a nonmoral reason: the avoidance of harm. The question of harm to himself is touched on later in the *Apology* in terms that Socrates knows will generate a wave of indignation among the jurors:

(S26) For you are to know well that if you kill me, being of the sort

I say I am [= innocent], you will not harm me more than yourselves. For neither Meletus nor Anytus would harm me at all. He couldn't even do so, for I do not think it is permitted [*themiton*, allowed by *themis*, the divine order of things] that a better man be harmed by a worse. Of course he could perhaps kill me or banish me or disfranchise me. Maybe he, and others perhaps, think that these are great evils, but I don't think so. [I think it is] much [worse] to do what he is doing now: attempting to have a man killed unjustly.[90]

There is a comparison here between the effect that one particular act would have on Socrates and what it would do to his accusers. Obviously, the mention of harm to his accusers in the event that their indictment is successful, and, moreover, a *greater* harm than the one to be inflicted on the accused, is surprising and paradoxical. Anyone hearing this for the first time would be inclined to think that it is absurd. Why should there be any harm to the victors? Socrates was right to anticipate general displeasure and a storm of protest on the part of the court.

Socrates' assertion is, however, perfectly intelligible, given certain basic assumptions. To harm someone is to do something that is bad for that person; i.e., to cause harm is to deprive a person of something that is good for her. The greater the good of which the person is deprived, the greater the harm inflicted. The comparison, therefore, between levels of resulting harm can be reduced to a comparison between the goods involved.

If Socrates is condemned, the evils he will suffer include death, exile, or the loss of his political rights (*atimia*). The corresponding goods are life, residence in the city, and the full exercise of rights in the *polis*.

Anyone will agree that these are, respectively, great evils and great goods. And yet Socrates thinks there is something much worse than these evils: to execute someone unjustly. In comparison, he holds, they are not as bad as this. To order an unjust execution is worse, in the nonmoral sense of "worse."

By implication and generalization, we arrive at the Socratic doctrine that among the greatest goods for an individual, are the exercise of justice and moral uprightness. In comparison, such good things as citizenship, life in the city, and even life itself, appear as small goods. Therefore, to be deprived of one of *these* is to suffer small harm. It follows that Socrates' accusers will suffer much greater harm.[91]

There is, then, a sharp difference between the scale of values or goods advocated by Socrates and that accepted by most Athenians.

What reasons does Socrates offer in defense of his position? In the *Apology*, of course, he offers none. It would be completely inappropriate for him to provide a detailed justification of the most general principles of his moral philosophy while defending himself in court. But a serious objection remains: to act in accordance with justice will, more often than not, harm rather than benefit the agent. It seems that the one who really benefits is not the agent himself, but rather the individual who is fortunate enough to have been treated honestly.

The thesis provisionally extracted from the *Apology* emerges here as a controversial and problematic cornerstone for the building we are trying to reconstruct:

> *The exercise of justice, i.e., of an excellence governed by respect for the good of others, is a fundamental good for oneself.*

Later we shall see how Plato places this Socratic conviction at the center of the *Gorgias;* and then, probably exceeding the boundaries of the philosophy of Socrates, how he writes the *Republic* as a grandiose *plaidoyer* in its defense.

But before looking at the *Gorgias*, we should consider another admirable document which shares with the *Apology* its representation of Socrates faced with a decision between life and death.

The *Apology* has given us a glimpse of a decision-making principle for action, and a sketch of a theory of goods or values. The *Crito* will confirm this initial attempt to identify the central elements of Socrates' moral philosophy.

III

Justifying a Decision: The *Crito*

Xenophon summarizes the theme of the *Crito* in a few lines from his *Apology*:

> Afterwards, when his companions wanted to steal and carry him off [from prison], he refused to follow them. He even seemed to make fun of them, asking them if they knew of any place outside of Attica [= the legal boundaries of the Athenian state] which was not accessible to death.[92]

The good intentions of Socrates' friends provide Xenophon with a renewed opportunity to depict the courage and sense of humor of the master in a simple and straightforward manner. In contrast, Plato's treatment of the same event leads to a complex and rigorous meditation on Socrates' reasons for rejecting a seemingly reasonable offer. Since Socrates is innocent of the charges that have led to his conviction, it would seem perfectly justifiable for him to flee.

Under normal circumstances, the execution of a criminal in ancient Athens would take place early on the day after the trial. A verdict of the people's court could not be appealed. In Socrates' case something unusual happens which delays the execution nearly thirty days.[93] We hear about it in the opening section of the *Phaedo*:

> (S27) Phaedo: A fortunate coincidence [τύχη] befell him, Echecrates, for it happened [ἔτυχεν] that the day before the trial the stern of the ship the Athenians send to Delos had been crowned.
> Echecrates: What ship is that?
> Phaedo: It is the ship, the Athenians say, in which Theseus once sailed to Crete with the "twice seven" [= seven youths and seven maidens sent by Athens to be sacrificed to the Minotaur, the mythi-

cal ruler of Knossos]. He saved them and he saved himself. According to the tale, they [= the Athenians] vowed to Apollo at the time that if they were saved, they would send a mission [*theoria*, a religious pilgrimage] to Delos [an island in the Aegean where Apollo and his sister Artemis had been born] every year. Ever since, down to the present day, they have always sent it annually to the god. They have a law that once the mission has started they are to keep the city pure and not execute anyone during the time required by the ship to reach Delos and return [= to Athens]. This sometimes takes a long time, if the winds happen [τύχωσιν] to detain them. The mission starts when the priest of Apollo crowns the stern of the ship, and this happened [ἔτυχεν] to have taken place, as I said, the day before the trial. Because of this Socrates spent a long time in prison between the trial and his execution.[94]

The opening scene of the *Crito* takes place before dawn in Socrates' cell on the day after the state galley has been sighted at Sounion, a promontory at the southernmost tip of Attica. The sacred ship will arrive at the Piraeus that very day.

Crito arrives at the crack of dawn, but allows his friend to go on sleeping comfortably. After Socrates awakens, they discuss the proposal which has motivated Crito's early visit, viz., the conspiracy to help Socrates escape from jail. Everything has been taken care of. The guards have been bribed, some foreigners have brought enough money to defray expenses, and Crito's friends in Thessaly will welcome Socrates and protect him, if he chooses to go there.[95]

Once more, because of Crito's good intentions, Socrates stands at a crossroads. Again he has the opportunity to choose between life and death.

Crito knows, of course, that Socrates will not leap at the offer to escape. He knows that Socrates must be persuaded, hence his eagerness to offer a host of arguments which can be roughly stated as follows:

(i) If Socrates allows himself to be executed, Crito will be deprived of an irreplaceable friend.

(ii) If Socrates allows himself to be executed, many will think that Crito was unwilling to spend money to save him, and hence has abandoned him.

(iii) If Socrates escapes, Crito will still be able to defend himself from the accusations made by sycophants or paid informers, and will not be forced to pay heavy fines or lose his property.

(iv) If Socrates allows himself to be executed, he will have done treason to himself, for he will have done what his enemies want him to do.

(v) If Socrates allows himself to be executed, he will have betrayed his sons by going away and leaving them instead of bringing them up and educating them.

(vi) If Socrates allows himself to be executed, he will show himself lacking the qualities of a good and courageous man. He will have given up the excellences for which he professed to care.

(vii) If Socrates allows himself to be executed, Crito and his friends will be thought of as incompetent and cowardly individuals.[96]

The upshot of these arguments is that Socrates' execution would not only be bad. It would also be morally shameful, both for him and for his friends.[97]

The arguments themselves are rather heterogeneous, and some of them are inextricably associated with certain moral conceptions. Let us take a closer look at the whole set.

Reason (i) is perhaps a simple and genuine expression of friendly affection.

Reasons (ii) and (iii) stress the subordinate value of money, but in a subtle way they probably have an effect quite opposite to the intended one. By insisting that the pecuniary loss will be minimal, Crito implicitly attributes to Socrates a concern for fluctuations in wealth that is alien to his character.

Reason (iii) assumes the context of Athenian democratic institutions, within which a private citizen could initiate a prosecution against a public offender (i.e., the right and duty to prosecute was not vested in specific magistrates required to act *ex officio*). Hence the practice arose of hiring a professional accuser or sycophant to bring charges against one's political rivals. A wealthy Athenian could thus bring his personal enemies to court without having to suffer the inconvenience of prosecuting in person.

Reasons (iv), (vi), and (vii) must be understood against the backdrop of heroic ethics, because their force flows from the opprobrium involved in the charge of worthlessness and cowardice (κακία, ἀνανδρία).[98] Furthermore, (iv) assumes that to do something in accordance with the intentions of an enemy is equivalent to treason, a more serious charge perhaps than that of weakness and unmanliness.

Crito's arguments (ii) and (vii) have to do with reputation and honor, but in (ii) the notion itself is a far cry from the τιμή, *time*, of the Homeric heroes. For them, *time* was first and foremost the recognition of a man's status and martial deeds by his peers, the other chieftains. Here we have instead "the opinion of the many," "the what-will-people-think" of a more egalitarian society.

Finally, the care for one's children expressed in (v) appeals to a universal duty not bound by any particular moral conception.

Socrates begins his reply to these arguments by making a general observation:

> (S28) We must examine whether this should be done [*prakteon*] or not, for I am, not now for the first time but always have been, the sort of man to be persuaded by nothing I possess other than the argument [*logos*, reason] which upon reasoning appears to me to be best. The arguments I have hitherto expressed I cannot now jettison [just] because of this fate that has befallen me. They appear to me as being practically equal [in force as before]. And I respect and honor the same ones as I did before. If we cannot now express something better than those arguments, you know well that I will not agree with you, not even if the power of the many scares us with more bogeys than it does at present, sending upon us incarcerations, executions, and confiscations of property.[99]

According to this passage, Socrates will make a decision in the light of the argument or reason that seems best to him. He does not expect this argument to be a sudden fancy of his, but rather one of those *logoi* which he has earlier conceived in the course of "open-ended discussions" (as I have called them). These reasons should not be abandoned in the present circumstances just because they entail unwelcome consequences.

This passage, then, tends to confirm in broad terms what we assumed in chapter I. In it Socrates openly declares that he is committed to a certain body of moral ideas. He is not willing to reject them *on the basis of fears*, but he is at all times willing to revise them *on the basis of good reasons*. He makes it clear indeed that he will stand by his convictions "if we cannot now express [*legein*] something better." If they were now able to formulate a better *logos* than those entertained in the past, he would be open to modifying his moral philosophy. That simply does not happen.

Socrates does mention the decisive role of the best argument in making a choice, but perhaps stressing the importance of this passage gives undue weight to a single aspect of his character, the rational aspect, while neglecting a different, yet also well-documented trait of his personality.

The Divine Sign

In the *Symposium*, for instance, we are told that during the siege of Potidaea, a city in northern Greece which had revolted from the Athenian empire in 432 B.C., Socrates spent over twenty-four hours standing in the same spot, totally oblivious to what was going on around him.

At first, this anecdote might suggest some form of ecstatic or religious experience, especially given that Socrates prays to the sun at the beginning of the new day; but on closer inspection the text indicates that his state of profound concentration is probably a result of his search for a solution to a strictly intellectual problem. The three participles that depict what he was up to clearly point in this direction (τι . . . σκοπόν, "examining something," ζητῶν, "searching," φροντίζων τι, "thinking about something").[100] Therefore, we should not assume that Socrates was undergoing something akin to a nonrational, mystical experience.

More directly relevant here are the frequent allusions to a unique nonrational factor in Socrates' decision making. Both in Plato and in Xenophon,[101] Socrates claims that some of his choices are guided by "the divine sign" (*to tou theou semeion, to daimonion semeion*, or simply *to daimonion*, "the divine (sign)," from *daimon*— not "demon" in its common meaning in English, but rather "god" or "divine being").[102] This sign, or voice (*phone*), as it is also called, is mentioned twice in the Platonic *Apology*:

(S29) The cause of this [= that I do not attempt to speak to the Assembly, that I am not an active participant in everyday politics] is something you have often heard me say in many places: that something divine and godlike happens to me. This is what Meletus has ridiculed in his written deposition. It started when I was still a child. It is like a voice that comes to me, and when it does, it always prevents me from doing what I am about to do. It never encourages [me to do something]. This is what prevents my becoming active in politics.[103]

After the vote that condemns him to death, Socrates explains:

(S30) Something amazing has happened [to me]. My habitual pro-
phetic [voice], the one from god, in the past has always [spoken to
me] very frequently and has very much opposed me in small matters, if I were about to do something incorrectly. Now something
has happened that you can see for yourselves, something which
anybody would consider, and which is generally regarded as ex-
tremely bad. And yet neither as I left home at dawn did the sign of
the god stand in my way, nor when I came up to the court, nor in
any way during my speech [*logos*] when I was about to say something. In other conversations [*logoi*], though, it has often held me
back in the middle of what I was saying. With regard to what I am
doing now, it has in no way opposed me, either in what I've done or
said. What do I suppose to be the cause of this? I will tell you. It may
be that what has befallen me is good, and that we who believe that
to die is bad cannot grasp it correctly. I have a great proof of this, for
it is impossible that the habitual sign would not have opposed me,
were I not about to do something good.[104]

Given the scant information provided by passages such as
these, it is not surprising that the interpretation of the divine sign
remains disputed and cannot perhaps be ultimately settled. Is it a
symptom of psychological abnormality or some pathological
state? Or should we view it as a genuine religious experience to be
explained as a form of communication with the divine? It is also
possible to conceive of the sign as nothing more than the normal
voice of moral conscience described in more striking terms.

Whether Socrates is reporting a pathological or a religious experience I am not in a position to decide, but I think it is possible to
show that the third conjecture, which views it the divine sign as
Socrates' moral conscience, must be discounted.

On a first reading, this view might seem correct, because in (S30)
the sign prevents Socrates from engaging in an activity described
by an expression that can be understood in a narrowly moral
sense: *me orthos prattein*, "to act incorrectly." The context, however, will allow us to infer that the reference is not to what is *morally* but rather *prudentially* incorrect.

The term "prudential" and its cognates, we should note, are
used in moral philosophy to qualify choices and actions from the
perspective of self-interest. If an action is beneficial to the agent or

results in something good for her in a nonmoral sense, we say that she has made a prudent choice. To engage in physical exercise on a regular basis and thus remain healthy is, in this sense, a prudent thing to do.

In (S29) the mysterious voice prevents Socrates from playing an active role in Athenian politics. Doing so would not have been morally wrong. In fact, toward the end of the Peloponnesian War, in 406—i.e., two years before the final defeat, when Athens had lost a sizable portion of its citizens—Socrates did accept membership in the Council or *Boule*.[105] Apparently this decision, late in his life and in light of the severe conditions in Athens, was made without objection on the part of the divine sign.

Socrates explains that the reason for the earlier opposition of the divine sign was that his strict adherence to standards of justice would have turned the majority against him (as it in fact did when he served in the Council). He might, as a result, have been killed much earlier, long before he had a chance to benefit himself and his fellow Athenians.[106] Considering the good of Athens and his own good (i.e., his attainment of the good life, as we shall see), it would not have been prudent for Socrates to go into politics.

The same rationale appears in (S34). Since it is generally thought that death is a great evil (in the nonmoral sense, i.e., that it is bad for the person who dies, regardless of any moral responsibility on his part or that of others), Socrates expected the sign to prevent him from going to a place where he would face the prospect of being condemned to die. Since the sign shows no opposition, Socrates concludes on the basis of his past experience that death is probably not bad for him. It may indeed be something good.[107]

None of the remaining references in Plato to the divine sign, I believe, can be construed as evidence supporting the view that it provided guidance for a choice between doing something morally right and doing something morally wrong.[108] We should conclude, therefore that in Plato's writings the function of the divine sign not only is negative, as (S29) and (S30) clearly show, it is exclusively prudential. It saves Socrates from nonmoral evils.

In Xenophon, on the other hand, the voice plays a positive role. It tells Socrates "what ought to be done" (ὅ τι χρὴ ποιεῖν),[109] or both what he ought and ought not to do (ἅ τε δέοι καὶ ἃ μὴ δέοι ποιεῖν).[110] The quoted expressions, by themselves, do not tell us whether they encourage or discourage action from a specific perspective. They can perfectly well cover both moral injunctions and prudential admonitions. It is possible, of course, that Xenophon simply misunderstands Socrates' remarks about his inner voice and thus lumps together two domains within his teacher's thought that Plato is able to sharply distinguish.

Perhaps more revealing is a rather extended defense of the *daimonion* in which Xenophon argues that it plays a role analogous to that of oracles, augury, and divination. There are matters the gods have reserved for themselves, he argues, for you may plant a field well, but not know who will gather the fruits; you may build a house well, but not know who will end up living in it; you may marry a pretty woman, and not know whether she will bring you sorrow; etc. None of these outcomes is clear to human beings. Indeed,

> (S31) if any man thinks that these matters are wholly within the grasp of the human mind [*gnome*] and nothing in them is divine [*daimonion*], then that man, he [= Socrates] said, is irrational [*daimonan*]. But it is no less irrational to seek the guidance of divination in matters which men are permitted by the gods to decide [*diakrinein*] for themselves by study [*mathousi*]: to ask, for instance, whether it is better to get an experienced coachman to drive my carriage or a man without experience, or whether it is better to get an experienced seaman to steer my ship or a man without experience. So too with what we may know by reckoning, measurement, or weighing. To put such questions to the gods seemed to his mind profane [*athemita*, unlawful, godless things]. In short, what the gods have granted us to do by help of learning, we must learn; what is hidden from mortals we should try to find out from the gods by divination.[111]

In other words, it is lawful to consult an oracle only if the query is about an unpredictable future event. Such consultation is senseless if we are asking about something we could know and anticipate through our own rational powers.

We must suppose, I think, that Xenophon's Socrates views moral decisions as falling under the second category. The moral attributes of action can hardly be taken as inscrutable future outcomes. Hence, oracles and divination are not necessary to discern if what one is about to do is right or wrong. This form of knowledge, similar to the crafts or *technai*, requires a certain amount of learning, after which it would be irrational to rely on religious sources that by their very nature are not expected to replace usual human reflection and foresight.

If this is correct, then Xenophon's interpretation of the divine sign is not substantially different from Plato's. The *daimonion* does not relieve Socrates of the need to voice rational moral judgments based on the reasons he has discussed throughout his life.

It is therefore natural that in the *Crito* Socrates should invoke the arguments he and his friend have accepted in the past, and that, if they are in conflict with reasons offered against them, he should abide by the argument that seems best to him. Such a decision-making procedure, then, will be a purely rational one; i.e., it appeals only to reasons that can be publicly explained to any reasonable interlocutor. What is thereby excluded is the appeal to, and admission of, a subjective and private authority, even if it is considered divine.

The examination of the role of the divine sign in determining the morality of Socrates' decisions has yielded similar results to those obtained when we examined the possibility of his ethics being a divine command theory. Socrates is willing to do something only because he rationally sees it to be instrinsically right.

The Reply to Crito

Let us return to Socrates' reply to Crito's arguments. At the outset, perhaps to clear the field, Socrates attacks the idea of allowing oneself to be influenced by "what people will say," by the opinion of the many.

Socrates' argument proceeds by analogy. In the domain of physical training and therapeutic dieting, we do not accept the opinion of the majority. We follow the instructions of the expert— i.e., the trainer or the physician—in questions of exercise or food intake, respectively. If we rely on what the ignorant majority tells us to do, we run the risk of suffering harm, of being deprived of a good.[112] In such cases the harm is to the body. It is corrupted and ruined by disease, and life is not worth living with one's body in bad condition.

This is the basis for the analogy. This section of the argument can be accepted without further ado because it is sufficiently obvious. From this set of relations Socrates projects a one-to-one correspondence to items in a different set.

Food and exercise correspond to "the just and the unjust, the shameful and the admirable, the good and the bad (deeds we can perform)."[113] These actions define a domain that is held analogous to the subject matter of medicine. Today we would call it "ethics." In the text the discipline itself is left unlabeled, but it is assumed that its social distribution corresponds to that of medicine: few are knowledgeable in it and "the many" are simply incompetent. We should therefore follow the advice "of a single individual, if there is someone who knows." Just as in matters pertaining to health and illness, following majority opinion may lead to harm.

The harm in this case would affect the item that within the analogy corresponds to the body and is identified descriptively by the expression "that which is harmed by the unjust and benefited by the just."[114] It is perhaps significant that the text omits the term one would expect to find here, namely "the soul" (*psyche*), a term which in Greek tradition often designates the principle of life and/or the seat of knowledge. The periphrastic description seems to suggest that, according to Socrates, there are only two fundamental components in human beings: the physical and the ethical. This is consistent with Socrates' lack of interest in contemplation or *theoria*. In his view, the intellectual powers of man are essentially practical and hence indissolubly tied to that which is affected by just or unjust acts in the same way the body is affected by wholesome food or poison.

The analogy concludes: just as life is not worth living when the body is ill, likewise life is unbearable when the seat of the moral dimension is ruined.[115] This conclusion seems counterfactual; it could be argued that there is no comparison between suffering pangs of conscience and bearing a debilitating and painful illness. It seems possible to live with, or even to repress, the recollection of an offense to justice which, for instance, resulted in considerable wealth and prosperity.

It should be noted, however, that Socrates does not seem to have in mind the sort of pain caused by remorse or feelings of guilt, i.e., by the subjective voice of inner moral conscience. The text suggests that the harm generated by one's injustice is an objective state, a state that can be inferentially discovered by an external observer on the basis of actions which take place in the public domain and are judged in the light of the excellences. Even if conscience's inner voice were to be silenced or repressed, the harm would still be there.

Fully consistent with this view are the efforts in the subsequent section of the *Crito* to determine criteria by which one could objectively judge the act of escaping from jail. Socrates formulates the problem as follows:

(S32) Therefore, from what we have agreed upon [ἐκ τῶν ὁμολογουμένων], we should examine whether it is just or unjust for me to try to escape from here without the consent of the Athenians. If it appears just, let us attempt it; if not, let us leave it at that. The observations you have made about loss of money or reputation, or the education of children, these I fear, Crito, are really considerations of those who would lightly kill and bring back to life, if they could, without giving much thought to it; I mean the many. Since the argument [the *logos*] proves it, we should consider only what we have just mentioned: whether we shall be doing what's just in giving money and thanks to those who will get me out of here, and ourselves leading and following in the escape, or whether we shall be truly acting unjustly in doing all of this. If it is clear to us that we would be acting unjustly in doing all of this, then we shouldn't take into account whether we must die by staying put and keeping calm, or whether we will suffer anything else, instead of acting unjustly [i.e., in preference to taking into account the avoidance of committing an unjust act].[116]

The terms employed by Socrates to formulate the question he and Crito are attempting to answer follow quite strictly the principle which in the preceding chapter is called (P3): the decision to stay or to flee should be made without taking into consideration any of the points invoked by Crito. It should be made exclusively in the light of the moral attributes of the act itself. This principle is now referred to simply as "the *logos*."

Determining the morality of the act of escaping, however, is by no means an easy task. There is, of course, a strong presumption favoring the view that it is right to flee on the grounds that the sentence itself is unfair, i.e., that Socrates is first and foremost the victim of an undeserved injustice. To escape would be simply to avoid a penalty that should not be imposed in the first place. Someone might even argue that it would be equivalent to the escape of a prisoner from a Nazi concentration camp.

In order to evaluate Socrates' paradoxical answer we must go over "the *logos* that seems to him to be the best." Its starting point is a principle which he and his friend have often entertained with approval and which amounts to rejecting a distinction between cases in which it would be licit to do wrong, i.e., to do something unjust, and cases in which it would not:

(P6) One should in no way do wrong.[117]

This principle derives its imperative force from a proposition asserted as true by Socrates both here and in (S16) which can now be stated more formally:

(P7) To do wrong is in every way bad and shameful.[118]

The derivation of (P6) from (P7) requires a further premise which does not appear explicitly in the text, perhaps because it simply marks the action-guiding force implicit in the terms corresponding to "bad" and "shameful" (below I shall further distinguish these two predicates):

(P8) The bad and the shameful should not be done.

In the section that follows the statement of (P6),[119] Socrates relies on this principle as a reason to reject a kind of action that most people would be inclined to treat as an exception to the rule, viz., the particular case in which an act of injustice is performed in return for an injustice suffered. General opinion, both now and then, favors the view that in such cases retribution is morally permissible. We usually label this kind of action "retaliation." It should be noted, however, that such actions do not include instances of legitimate punishment imposed, after a fair trial, by a competent authority. An appropriate example would be the execution of several hostages for each of our soldiers killed in an ambush, or the bombing of a civilian population after the enemy has bombed our civilians.

The defining characteristic of these examples, and of retaliation in general, is that the harm inflicted in retribution does not fall upon the individuals who are directly responsible for the initial aggression. This feature determines the injustice of retaliation: the innocent are punished by association.

That Socrates is sternly opposed to such practices becomes clear when he requests Crito's assent to:

(P9) One should not do wrong in return for having suffered wrong.

The justification of (P9), as we saw, is to be found in (P6), because (P9) is a simple application of the universal principle to the particular case of retaliation. If it is true that one should *never* do wrong, then it follows that one should not do wrong in specific cases, such as making the innocent pay for the guilty.

Crito's acceptance of (P9) marks an important step in the decision-making procedure, because it brings out the fact that the injustice of the verdict is totally irrelevant in discerning the key issue. The moral attributes of the act of escaping must be ascertained independently of the justice or injustice of the sentence passed by the court.

After a clarification of what is meant by "injustice" ("to harm a human being," "to do something that is bad for humans," κακῶς ποιεῖν ἀνθρώπους),[120] Socrates asks whether or not his friend still holds the following principle:

(P10) Just agreements ought to be fulfilled.

This principle implies that it would be unjust not to honor an agreement (ὁμολογία, συνθήκη), provided that the agreement is just. This last clause may seem to introduce a redundancy, but the reference to the justice of the agreement is actually located at a different level. Its point is surely to rule out as morally binding those agreements or contracts which are unfair either because of the circumstances under which they were made (e.g., under duress, or in ignorance of the contents, etc.) or because their point is itself unjust (e.g., to rob or murder someone). Such defects are sufficient for annulment of the corresponding contract. And it would obviously not be unjust to violate a contract that was null and void.

From the clarification of the meaning of "unjust" and from (P10) it follows that an action can be unjust either because it consists in harming someone or because it is actually in violation of an agreement, or both. This explains why Socrates' reformulation of the central question about escaping takes both possibilities into account:

> (S33) If we leave this place not having persuaded the city, shall we or shall we not be harming people whom we should least harm? Shall we or shall we not be keeping our just agreements?[121]

Rather than encouraging Crito to offer replies to each of these questions and then showing by means of the *elenchos* that they are defective, Socrates resorts to a rhetorical device which is unparalleled in the early dialogues. Instead of arguing *about* the laws that require him to remain in prison, he asks Crito to imagine the laws themselves appearing in his cell and delivering a lengthy speech in defense of their injunctions. In later rhetorical theory this is called "prosopopoeia," or personification.[122]

The reaction of the laws to the first question is as follows:

> (S34) Tell me, Socrates, what do you intend to do? By this action you are attempting, don't you intend to destroy us the laws as far as you are concerned? Do you suppose a city can survive and not be subverted if the verdicts of its courts have no force and are nullified and destroyed by private individuals?[123]

Socrates then adds on his own:

> (S34 cont.) What shall we reply to these and to similar [questions], Crito? Anyone, but especially an orator [= a citizen appointed to function as public defender of a law that is to be abrogated], would have much to say in defense of this law we are destroying which requires that the verdicts of the courts remain in force.[124]

The reasoning deployed here by the laws has often been interpreted as a consequentialist argument, i.e., an argument that invokes the (bad) consequences of an act to declare that the act itself is morally wrong. In this case, the inadmissible outcome would be the destruction of the city, which in turn would follow from the destruction of the laws. This reasoning also requires generalized disobedience for the undesirable consequence actually to follow. Under this interpretation, it is morally wrong for an individual to violate the law, because if *everyone* violated the law, then the city would be destroyed.[125]

If this is the argument Socrates attributes to the laws, then Crito should not have been persuaded. It can be granted that massive disobedience of the law will fatally harm the political community, but it does not seem to be true that if one individual violates a particular law, then all the citizens will violate (all?) the laws. On the contrary, one could even argue that Socrates' escape would have been a minimal violation, which, moreover, was in Athens' best interest. At least the city would have benefited from avoiding the opprobrium of going down in history as the renowned Greek *polis* which executed one of its most eminent philosophers.

This main weakness of the argument under the proposed interpretation is that it makes a questionable assumption of generalization in ethics. It assumes that the moral judgment depends on the factual question of whether or not, from the act of one individual, a deluge of similar acts will follow. Alternatively, a nonconsequentialist understanding of generalization holds that if something is licit for one individual, it will also be licit for all similarly situated individuals, whether or not they do in fact perform the act. On this view, if it is morally right for Socrates to escape from jail, it will also be right for any Athenian who has been condemned in similar circumstances.

Generalization is doubtless an important ingredient in the speech of the laws, but which of the two views of generalization should we attribute to Socrates? The question will allow us to decide whether or not Socratic ethics as such should be understood as a consequentialist system of ethics.

A Consequentialist Theory?

It must be granted that, by focusing on the destruction of the city, the wording of (S34) does suggest a consequentialist approach. Indeed, it would seem that this passage contradicts principle (P3), the decision-making principle which exhorted the agent to disregard the consequences of a given action.

On closer scrutiny, though, it can be shown that the two views are not inconsistent. According to (P3), the consequences that should not be taken into account are the good or bad consequences *for oneself*, while in (S34), the consequences taken into account are the effects an act will have *on someone else*, viz., on the body of the citizens of Athens. It should be clear that Socrates is holding that this latter outcome *ought* to be considered.

Whether or not consequences must be taken into consideration is therefore not an open question. Rather, the question is whether or not they constitute the *sole criterion* for determining the morality of an act.

(S34) contains enough elements to suggest a negative reply to this question, a reply based on the notion of harm and subsequently confirmed by the argument based on the notion of contract or agreement.

In (S34) the laws ask Socrates: "What do you intend to do?" (τί ἐν νῷ ἔχεις ποιεῖν; "What do you have in mind to do?"). They refer to "this action you are attempting" (τούτῳ τῷ ἔργῳ ᾧ ἐπιχειρεῖς) and they ask what he "intends to do" (διανοῇ, "thinks [he] will do"), "as far as [he] is concerned" (τὸ σὸν μέρος). These expressions jointly suggest that in order to specify the kind of action at hand, and hence to be able to pass judgment upon it, it is essential to determine the thoughts that embody Socrates' *intentions*.

By attempting to escape, Socrates intends to disobey a single judicial verdict. The laws show him that to intend to do this is equivalent to intending to destroy them and the city. But this must be justified. How can intention to disobey in one case be equated with intention to harm and destroy in all cases? This, I believe, is a correct yet misleading way to pose the question.

The function of the general consideration is to contribute to the argument a criterion to decide what Socrates will be doing in this particular case. Laws and judicial decisions discharge their social role if they are in fact enforced. Disobedience amounts to depriving them of their force, to stripping them of their authority.[126] According to the text, this is equivalent to their destruction.[127] A disobeyed order will have suffered an extreme form of harm. If the political community is defined by its laws,[128] then harm to the laws logically entails harm to the city. The argument, therefore, does not depend on future, empirically verifiable, outcomes. If Socrates intends to disobey a particular court order, and if to disobey it is to inflict harm on the verdict itself and by implication on the city and the citizens, it follows that the act itself would be wrong, regardless of what other people might do. The harm would surely be more obvious and visible if disobedience became a common practice, but it is already present in one singular act.

If this interpretation is correct, confirmation has been found for an idea which has been gradually emerging and which constitutes the core of Socratic ethics: the idea that the acts themselves, and not their eventual consequences, are endowed with the attributes that determine their moral quality.

The Contract with the City

Let us return to the main line of argument. If, because of the very nature of the intended act, escaping from jail produces harm, and if producing harm is always unjust, it logically follows that it would be unjust for Socrates to flee.

In the text, however, the matter is not yet settled. There is an almost imperceptible transition from the argument relying on the injustice of inflicting harm to the argument which is based on the premise following from (P10), i.e., that it is unjust to violate fair agreements or contracts.[129]

For this argument to be plausible, there must have been a contract in which Socrates was one of the parties. Accordingly, the rest of the speech of the laws is designed to show that Socrates' actual behavior in Athens proves that he entered into a tacit agreement with the city. In its most relevant sections it reads:

(S35) "Consider then, Socrates," the laws would probably say, "whether what we say is true: namely that what you intend to do to us now is unjust. In fact, we gave you birth, we nourished you, we educated you, giving you and all other citizens a share in all the good things [*kala*] of which we were capable. We proclaimed nevertheless the freedom [*exousia*, permission] to leave for any Athenian who wishes it, after he has become a full citizen and has observed public affairs and us the laws. If he is not pleased with us, he is free to leave and go wherever he wants, taking his property with him. [. . .] We hold that whoever of you stays, observing how we conduct our lawsuits and manage the rest of the city's affairs, that individual has already reached a *de facto* agreement with us [ὡμολογηκέναι ἔργῳ ἡμῖν] to do whatever we order him to do. We also hold that whoever disobeys us does wrong [ἀδικεῖν, commits injustice] in three ways. For although we are [a] his parents and [b] his guardians, he disobeys us, and [c] having agreed [ὁμολογήσας] to obey us, he neither obeys nor persuades us, if we do something wrong [μὴ καλῶς, not rightly]. We propose [alternatives] and do not issue savage orders to do what we command. We allow one of two things,

either to persuade us or to do [what we say], and yet he does neither
of the two. To such charges we hold that you will be liable, Socrates,
if you do what you intend to do [ἃ ἐπινοεῖς], and you not least
among the Athenians, but most of all." Should I say to them, "How
so?" they would rightly [δικαίως, justly] upbraid me, saying that
more than any other Athenian, I happen to have agreed with them
on this contract [αὐτοῖς ὡμολογηκὼς τυγχάνω ταύτην τὴν ὁμολογίαν].
"Socrates," they would add, "we have substantial proof that you
like us and the city, for you would not have remained in her more
than any other Athenian, if you didn't exceedingly like her. You
have never left the city on a sacred mission [or to go sightseeing, ἐπὶ
θεωρίαν], except once to the isthmus [of Corinth, where athletic con-
tests in honor of Poseidon were held], nor have you gone to any
other place, unless you were going on military service, nor did you
ever travel abroad, as other men do. The desire to see other cities or
other laws never got hold of you. We and our city were enough for
you. So forcefully did you choose us and agree to be governed by
us. You also had children in the city, thereby showing that you were
pleased with it. Moreover, during the trial itself you could have
proposed exile as penalty, if you so wished, and would have thus
been able to do then with the approval of the city what you now
attempt to do with her disapproval. At that time you boasted that
you would not be vexed if you had to die, and you chose, as you
said, death in preference to exile. But now those words do not make
you feel ashamed, nor do you have any regard for us the laws since
you attempt [ἐπιχειρῶν] to destroy us. You are doing what the worst
slave would do, trying [ἐπιχειρῶν] to escape in violation of the pacts
and agreements [παρὰ τὰς συνθήκας τε καὶ τὰς ὁμολογίας] by which
you agreed [συνέθου] to be governed. First, then, tell us whether or
not we speak the truth when we hold that you have agreed
[ὡμολογηκέναι], by your deeds [ἔργῳ] though not by your words
[λόγῳ], to be governed by us."[130]

I have translated a rather lengthy portion of the speech of the
laws so that we may have a better view of its strengths and weak-
nesses. On the one hand, there is an almost disproportionate emphasis on the idea of an agreement, as the repetition of the
corresponding Greek terms shows. Socrates' whole life is interpreted as a proof of something that did not strictly take place, at
least in any explicit sense. Socrates did not sign a contract with
Athens. The contract is a tacit one. Since Socrates has received
many benefits from Athens, it is argued that he has made a com-

mitment to obey the law in exchange for those benefits.

Justifying obedience to the law is a difficult topic requiring a lengthy discussion within which Socrates would have been expected to make abundant use of the *elenchus*. Moreover, the question itself could only have been resolved in the light of a definition of justice. But the dramatic setting of the *Crito* does not allow the length of time needed for a prolonged series of exchanges, nor would it have been appropriate for Plato to present Socrates accepting a settled definition of one of the cardinal virtues. Socrates, thus deprived of his peculiar irony, would have been totally out of character.

This explains, I believe, why the starting point for the argument that is given distinct prominence in the text is the kind of obligation that arises out of voluntary commitments. Acceptance of (P10) ("Just agreements ought to be fulfilled"), i.e., of the principle that governs voluntary undertakings, does not seem to Crito and Socrates to require further justification. It is assumed that any reasonable person will admit that it is true. In this sense, it is a piece of moral knowledge that is on a par with Socrates' claim in the *Apology* to *know* that disobeying one's superior or commanding officer is wrong.

If starting from voluntary obligation has strategic advantages over starting, say, from a natural obligation to obey the law, the strength of the proof depends on the plausibility of making civic duties a subset of one's voluntary obligations. Ultimately, the argument of the laws rests on something like a "love it or leave it" injunction. Since any citizen is free to leave, it follows that if he stays he has made a voluntary decision to accept all of the assets and all of the liabilities that go with life in the city. Chief among the latter, of course, is obedience to the law even when it commands actions that may lead to physical harm or even death.

Socrates and Civil Disobedience

A further difficulty is whether or not the laws demand total submission on the part of Socrates or, for that matter, on the part of any citizen. On this view it would seem that the laws could legitimately enforce obedience even in those cases where they command something unjust. It could be further suggested that the laws themselves determine what is just and what is unjust. If so, they could not, in principle, issue unjust commands. Neither of these two interpretations of the demands imposed by the laws (submission to all of them, including unjust ones, and submission to all of them because there are no unjust laws) would leave room for morally justified disobedience.

Let us try to address these problems, keeping in mind the particular case at hand.

On the basis of clear textual evidence, we have to reject at the outset the hypothesis that the laws might claim to offer exceptionless criteria for justice. They explicitly admit that they could be wrong ("if we do something which is not rightly done"),[131] that is, they admit the possibility of an unjust norm.

Should Socrates decide to escape from jail, however, his disobedience would not be the result of a decision to challenge an unjust law. This is made clear toward the end of the speech of the laws in a sentence that explains who, exactly, is responsible for the injustice done to Socrates:

> (S36) But now, if you leave, you will leave having been wronged [ἠδικημένος, having suffered an injustice] not by us, the laws, but by men.[132]

According to this, the injustice to Socrates was not caused by the laws as such, but by the jurors who condemned him for a crime he had not committed. Their behavior, however, was strictly in accordance with the norm that a juror is free to vote as he sees fit. The verdict was unjust, but not illegal.

Socrates, in fact, seems to regard Athenian procedural law as a body of just legal norms, whereas we would consider it seriously deficient because of its lack of safeguards. In ancient Athens, a defendant did not have the right to appeal a sentence passed swiftly by a mass of citizens (500, or 501 in the case of Socrates) who could easily have fallen prey to passion and prejudice. The system had no mechanisms for maximizing the chances of reaching a just verdict. It left ample room for someone to suffer an injustice.

The laws do insist on one feature of the system, however, which mitigates the apparent demand of total submission. It is expressed by the disjunction "persuade or obey," repeated three times during the speech to mark its importance.[133]

The exact meaning of the disjunction has been subject to scholarly controversy, but the following observations will not, I hope, be completely off the mark.

First, on a candid reading of the text, it seems that the disjunction is to be understood as presenting two mutually exclusive commands. You ought to either persuade or obey; that is, if you fail to obey, you should persuade, and if you fail to persuade, you should obey.[134] To do neither of the two is blameworthy.

Who is to be persuaded? The city, of course; but through which of its institutional organs? The idea used to be favored that the laws meant to encourage the citizen either to obey a particular statute or to work for the peaceful change of that same statute at a regular meeting of the Assembly; i.e., to make use of the legislative privilege of Athenian citizenship to repeal a law deemed unjust. The text does not explicitly mention the Assembly, but it does include a reference to the courts,[135] which is certainly more appropriate to Socrates' predicament. Hence, the disjunction probably reflects the right of an Athenian to be heard in court. During a trial, the defendant has the opportunity to persuade the jury "as to the nature of the just"[136] (a necessary premise for showing that in this particular instance he has not done anything unjust or committed a crime). But this, of course, can fail, in which case obedience is required.

Finally, the obedience component of the disjunction is narrowed down in this context to those orders which, if obeyed, carry with them negative consequences for the citizen. The examples given are quite eloquent. Obedience is due the city even if this leads the loyal citizen to suffer blows and bonds, wounds and death.[137] The implication is, of course, that having failed to persuade the jury, Socrates should obey the legal verdict that requires him to stay in prison and face execution, just as in warfare he was expected to obey the order not to abandon his post even at the risk of death.[138]

Because he is innocent, Socrates' obedience will lead him to suffer wrong; but how, one might ask, would he react to an order to do wrong? According to the *Apology*, Socrates' moral philosophy certainly had the conceptual resources to challenge commands requiring him to commit an act of injustice. As we saw, he declined to participate in the arrest of Leon of Salamis because, he argued, arrest followed by execution without trial is unjust.[139] It could be objected, however, that since the Thirty tyrants did not hold power lawfully, their command should not be seen as an order emanating from the city and thus subject to the "persuade or obey" doctrine.

It seems, however, that Socrates is also willing to defy an order that can be construed as legal, if it forces him to engage in unjust action. An example is the hypothetical injunction to refrain from philosophizing alluded to in (S24). Strictly speaking, the court cannot hand down conditional sentences acquitting a defendant on the condition of some future behavior; but Socrates' reply may be taken to address a broader possibility which is readily envisaged by the reader of the *Apology*: The Assembly could pass a law banning the practice of philosophy under penalty of death.[140] In the event of such a political decision, Socrates states that he would disobey. He says he would obey Apollo and continue to philosophize, in spite of the threats, for he *knows* that to disobey the god would be an instance of injustice on his part.[141]

The fact that we had to return to the *Apology* in search of a clue as to how Socrates would have reacted to a legal order to do wrong lends some initial plausibility to the view that the two writings offer opposing conceptions of obedience. On this view the *Crito* embodies an authoritarian notion of obedience to the law, whereas the *Apology* represents a more liberal one; hence there is a sharp contradiction between the two writings.[142] I do not think this line of thought is very promising, because the instance that prompts a statement on disobedience in the *Apology* is not considered at all in the *Crito*. In the private conversation between the two friends in Socrates' cell, the dramatic setting leaves no room to raise the hypothetical question of obedience to legal injunctions which require unjust action. Moreover, such obedience is implicitly ruled out by the explicit proviso that an agreement (and, *a fortiori*, Socrates' agreement with Athens) will be binding only if it is just. No agreement that demands an unjust deed can be itself just.

The speech of the laws, then, should not be read as an exhortation to blindly obey positive law. Some legal injunctions may be unjust, and some just legal rules may be inadequate to prevent unjust outcomes in particular cases. In the case of the *Crito*, a citizen has the opportunity to rectify an injustice, but if he fails, he must obey the order to undergo punishment. It would be unjust for him to harm the city by violating a law he has agreed to obey—

in this case, the basic norm that court decisions must be carried out. As (P9) made clear, suffering an injustice does not justify committing one.

Socrates' conclusion, then, is that he ought to stay and die. He derives this conclusion from the reply given to the question: "Is it just or unjust to escape?" The two branches of the argument, viz. one that rejects harm to others and one that rejects violations of fair agreements, lead to the same conclusion: it would indeed be unjust to escape.

Socrates' First Principles

If our interpretation of the *Crito* came to an end here, we would perhaps be willing to admit that Socrates remained faithful to (P3), since he took into consideration only the inherent moral quality of escaping from prison in making up his mind. But we may also feel inclined to view Socrates' ethics as strictly deontological. The ultimate justification for his not escaping, presented so far, is that escaping would be contrary to his moral duty.

Therefore, it is of the utmost importance to consider what led Socrates to frame the question in those terms. The dialogue proceeds as follows:

> (S37) (in part = S19 and S32) Soc.: But, my admirable friend, this argument [*logos*] we have gone through still seems to me to be the same as it did before. Examine in turn the following one [to see] if it still holds good for us or not, namely that it is not to live [τὸ ζῆν] that should be deemed most important, but to live well [τὸ εὖ ζῆν].
> Crito: It holds good.
> Soc.: And that [to live] well [εὖ] and finely [καλῶς] and justly [δικαίως] are the same, does this hold good or does it not hold good?
> Crito: It does hold good.
> Soc.: Therefore [οὐκοῦν, *ergo*], from what we have agreed upon [ἐκ τῶν ὁμολογουμένων], we should examine whether it is just or unjust for me to try to escape from here without the consent of the Athenians.[143]

The inferential expressions in this passage make it quite clear that the question concerning the morality of the plan proposed by Crito and his friends is raised *as a consequence* of the acceptance of certain principles. Those principles were accepted in the past and are still considered true. The first of them is:

(P11) Not life, but the good life, ought to be valued above all else.

In perfect consistency with the doctrine of goods sketched in the *Apology*, this thesis does not consider life to be one of the greatest goods. Better than life is a life of a certain quality, indeed of the best possible quality. But when is a human life a good life or, better still, an excellent life? The expression "the good life" is as ambiguous in English as it is in Greek. The average person, both then and now, thinks of it as a pleasant life, sustained by abundant wealth and a good reputation, and allowing for a wide variety of satisfactions.

Socrates differs from his contemporaries in his understanding of what constitutes the good life. He expresses it in the second principle mentioned in (S37):

(P12) The good life is the noble and just life.

This principle, as it appears in the text, is marked by a subtle transition from an expression whose primary sense is not moral ("the good life") to one which combines both a nonmoral and a moral connotation ("the good/beautiful life," "the admirable life," "the noble life"), and, finally, to one in which the moral flavor is uppermost ("the just life," "the morally upright life"). Plato's literary purpose is doubtless to ease the way for the reader to accept the paradoxical Socratic identification of the moral and the non-moral good.

We can now see that the claims expressed by (P11) and (P12) are diametrically opposed to the view that, by his willingness to suffer wrong, Socrates may have endorsed a moral philosophy which entails the radical renunciation of one's rights and happiness. Quite the contrary. All persons should try to secure for themselves the available goods. That is what valuing "the good life" entails. And to do so is highly rational.

The search for one's own good, then, is at the cornerstone of Socrates' moral philosophy. But equally fundamental is his conviction that the majority have a mistaken conception of what the good things are and of which things truly benefit us. In these matters, error and self-deception tend to predominate, because if

Socrates is right, we are placed under rather stringent demands. Our search for happiness becomes a continual effort to perform all of our actions in conformity with strict moral standards. In fact, (P12) can be paraphrased in a way that makes this clear:

(P13) Something is good for an agent if and only if it is morally right.

Now we are in a better position to understand why Socrates believes that raising the question of whether or not it would be moral to escape follows from the two previous principles he and Crito have agreed upon. If escaping is right, then it is something good for him. If it is wrong, then it is something bad for him. The moral evils are what is truly bad. The moral goods are the true goods. Given that Socrates, like any rational agent, wishes to attain what is good for him, it follows then that not only would it be wrong for him to escape, but it would also be stupid, because he would be depriving himself of a very important good. The quality of his life would be destroyed.

If this line of reasoning is correct, then the moral question raised in the *Crito* is subordinated to the prudential question, the consideration of one's own good or benefit. This allows us to infer with a high degree of confidence that Socrates' moral philosophy is not deontological, for it is *not* ultimately grounded on the imperative to do one's duty regardless of the ensuing good or evil for oneself. But it turns out not to be strictly teleological either, because the right is *not* defined as that which is conducive to an independently defined nonmoral good.[144]

At this stage of our inquiry, then, the sole constituent of Socratic happiness appears to be the morally upright life. Interpreting the *Crito* along these lines is a first step toward taking sides in the dispute concerning the question of the relation between virtue and happiness in Socratic ethics. We should accept, at least provisionally, that with regard to this question, (P12) and its reformulation as (P13) entail what has been called the coincidental interpretation, which excludes the instrumental one. The practice of the virtues is not, according to Socrates, a means to attain happiness. Virtue is not conducive to happiness. It *is* happiness. This thesis will be further refined in the next chapter in light of Socrates' views about certain nonmoral goods which have not yet been considered.

It should be noted that our interpretations of the *Crito* have uncovered a new Socratic paradox. By his actions and by his arguments, Socrates shows that if he escapes and continues to live, he will destroy his good life; and if he stays and dies, he will have attained the good life.

This and other perplexities will be further encountered in the *Gorgias* and considered in the next chapter.

IV

The Confrontation with Polus

The *Gorgias* is unique among the Platonic writings because of its dramatic tension. It would be interesting to know what led Plato to write an extensive dialogue in which Socrates faces individuals who, unlike Crito, are drastically opposed to his views. Perhaps we might imagine that Plato, while reflecting on the basic insights of Socratic ethics in order to teach them in the Academy, felt the need to defend those insights from certain objections which were probably becoming more common. It is not hard to see why some people would have raised such objections, either during Socrates' lifetime or in the decades after his death. His moral philosophy must have struck some of his listeners as counterintuitive. Indeed, its basic tenets seem radically opposed to those of the common man. In the *Gorgias* we encounter characters who are deeply irritated by the Socratic theses and who react with considerable animosity to this mode of thought whose lack of realism they consider to be dangerously deceptive. One character states that if what Socrates holds is true, then the life of every human being is really upside down: we are doing exactly the opposite of what we should.[145] And, he implies, this radical criticism of our practices is intolerable.

As the conversation moves forward, it becomes increasingly clear how difficult it is to defend the ethics Socrates advocates. Its most characteristic ingredients are its foundations, but Socrates does not attempt to justify them deductively. Hence, it might seem that the only way of commending those principles to others would be by appeal to a different strategy, e.g., pointing to the consequences that follow from living one's life in accordance with such principles. But it could be argued that those consequences tend to be disastrous. Indeed, chief among them was the execution of Socrates.

71

It is perhaps due to this realization that Plato invests a considerable amount of philosophical energy in the *Gorgias*, attempting not
so much to defend Socrates as to refute the positions of those who
oppose him. The main strategy aims at showing that the opposers
hold inconsistent views.

Toward the end of the dialogue, however, Plato has Socrates
make an unexpected move. We encounter an argument carefully
crafted to prove *deductively* that (12a)—i.e., that moral excellence is
the real human good—is true. As we shall see in chapter V, one of
the starting points of Socratic ethics ceases to be an axiom and
becomes a theorem. I shall also attempt to show that we cannot
reasonably attribute this new foundational strategy to the historical Socrates.

The structure of the *Gorgias* is relatively simple. Apart from
occasional interventions by a few minor figures, Socrates faces in
succession three main interlocutors. The first is the great sophist
Gorgias from Leontini in Sicily.[146] The discussion continues with a
Sicilian student of Gorgias, Polus of Acragas (or Agrigento),[147]
until he is relieved by a wealthy and brilliant young Athenian,
Callicles of Acharnae.[148] The dialogue comes to a close with a myth
on the judgment of the dead narrated by Socrates.[149]

After a brief look at the exchange between Socrates and Gorgias,
we shall focus our attention on the confrontation with Polus.

The initial topic of the dialogue is rhetoric, a skill that Gorgias
professes to teach and whose aim is to persuade. When Socrates
presses him to state what exactly it is that he teaches, Gorgias ends
up contradicting himself.

Initially, Gorgias holds that he trains students in a morally neutral skill, that is, in a skill that can be put to good or to bad use.
Hence, the teacher of rhetoric should not be blamed if his students
misuse the powerful tool they have acquired.[150] But later on,
Gorgias grants that he will not be able to teach rhetoric at all, unless the student knows in advance the truth about "the just and the
unjust, the shameful and the noble, the good and the bad."[151] If the
student is ignorant of such things, Gorgias admits that the student
will learn them from him as well.[152]

The reason for his concession is Gorgias' realization that the
effective exercise of rhetoric requires a good grasp of these fundamental evaluative notions, but Socrates takes him one step further

by asking him to grant that just as knowledge of what pertains to a craft makes one an expert in the corresponding craft, likewise knowledge of "the things that are just" makes one just.[153] The admission that he will teach "the just" to his students as a necessary condition for learning rhetoric entails that, having become just, no student of Gorgias will misuse the rhetorical skill he has learned. But this conclusion is at odds with the earlier understanding of rhetoric as a morally neutral craft.

When this inconsistency becomes clear, Polus rudely intervenes and attacks Socrates for having led Gorgias to contradict himself.[154] Shortly thereafter, in a surprising turn in the conversation, Socrates asks Polus whether he wants to ask questions or answer them, and Polus seizes the opportunity to lead the way. This exchange of roles is quite new and has no parallel in the earlier dialogues. The net result of this shift is that Socrates, functioning for the time being[155] as the one who provides the replies, can drop his habitual irony and express his own convictions.

Socrates states explicitly that rhetoric is not a craft (τέχνη), but a knack (ἐμπειρία, a practice based on experience) whose aim is to gratify and please the audience. Like its counterpart, cookery, its goal is to produce pleasure (ἡδονή). In contrast, a craft must satisfy two conditions:

(1) it must aim at something good—indeed, at the best—and not merely at what happens to be pleasant; and

(2) it must involve a rational procedure. Its practitioner has to have a *logos* or rational understanding of the nature of his object and of that which he applies to it. Only then can he explain the reason why he does what he does.[156]

Medicine is the clearest example of a craft. It aims at the restoration of the patient's health, which is doubtless a good, and it can explain why it prescribes a specific kind of drug for a specific patient and not a different one. The physician knows both the nature of the patient's illness and the nature of the medicine he is prescribing.

In an unusually long speech where Socrates sets forth the criteria for *techne*, he also presents a systematic classification of crafts and knacks dealing with the body and the soul.[157] It can be illustrated as follows:

CARE OF THE BODY

	Regulative (healthy body)	Corrective (sick body)
Craft	*gymnastics*	*medicine*
Form of flattery	*cosmetics*	*cookery*

CARE OF THE SOUL

	Regulative (healthy soul)	Corrective (sick soul)
Craft	*legislation*	*justice*
Form of flattery	*sophistry*	*oratory*

This classification displays a rigorous system of analogies or proportions (e.g., just as the art of medicine aims at curing the sick body, likewise justice, i.e. the *techne* of the judge, aims at restoring the health of the sick soul). But Polus shows no interest in understanding the classification and its interpretation, nor in defending his trade from the humorous charge of being analogous to the trade of cooks, i.e., of being a form of flattery. He wants to get right to what he sees as the heart of the matter. In his opinion, the decisive fact is that good orators are held in high regard and have the greatest power in their respective cities.[158]

Rhetoric and Power

The sense of Polus' remark needs to be understood within the context of a direct democracy, the system that prevailed in Athens during most of the fifth century. The Greek expression for "good orator" denoted the man who was able to persuade his fellow citizens in the Courts and in the Assembly. In the latter case, he was able to block decisions he opposed and to pass the measures he favored. The perfectly successful orator was the one who *always* carried the vote and whose will was invariably done. Polus, expressing perhaps his own political preference, compares the good orator to a tyrant, an individual who governs without any constitutional limitations.[159]

Polus, then, is emphasizing the key advantage of learning the craft Gorgias professes to teach and on which Polus himself has already written a treatise: rhetoric is conducive to the possession of power.[160]

As usual, Socrates' reaction is paradoxical. He holds that, on the contrary, orators have the least power in the city! Polus thinks this is ridiculous (and so may the reader). Accordingly, the dialogue develops an argument to show that Socrates' view, in spite of its apparent absurdity, is indeed justifiable. The argument requires initial agreement between the parties, which Socrates readily secures. By submitting for Polus' consideration an important property of power, Socrates claims that orators do not have the greatest power in the cities,

(S38) . . . if you call having power [τὸ δύνασθαι, the having of power] something good [ἀγαθόν τι] for the one who has it [τῷ δυναμένῳ, the powerful individual].[161]

Polus agrees without further ado because this characterization of power coincides with the standard opinion about what goes on in the real world: the powerful invariably use their power to benefit themselves. Indeed, many people at the time thought that declining to take advantage of a position of power was simply a sign of weakness.[162]

On this interpretation of (S38), it seems strange that Socrates should be the one to propose and affirm such a thesis. It will soon become clear, however, that Polus and Socrates have very different views about what falls under the key concept in this characterization of power, namely the concept of the good.

Polus defends his conviction that orators or influential politicians are powerful by raising a factual question:

(S39) Don't they, like tyrants, execute whomever they want [ὃν ἂν βούλωνται], and deprive him of his property and expel from their cities whoever seems [best] to them [ὃν ἂν δοκῇ αὐτοῖς]?[163]

In these lines, which exemplify the typical conception of unrestricted political power, Polus employs two expressions synonymously. Socrates immediately distinguishes between the two, holding that one of them is true of orators and tyrants while the other one is not:

(i) to do what seems to them to be best (ὅτι ἂν αὐτοῖς δόξῃ βέλτιστον εἶναι), and

(ii) to do what they want (ἃ βούλονται).[164]

Surprisingly, Socrates holds that tyrants and orators satisfy predicate (i), but not (ii). This paradox, as we shall presently see, is resolved by the introduction of a nonstandard definition of the verb "to want" (βούλεσθαι). In ordinary language, both Greek and English, we say that we want anything we do voluntarily. When a tyrant issues an order sending a political opponent into exile, it would be odd to say that he did not want to expel his opponent, particularly since the tyrant is not under any sort of mandate.

Socrates paves the way for removal of the oddity by first distinguishing what agents do [ὃ ἂν πράττωσιν] from the goal they wish to achieve [ἐκεῖνο οὗ ἕνεκα πράττουσιν τοῦθ' ὃ πράττουσιν, "that for the sake of which they do this that they do"].[165] Thus, for example, when we take a medicine that tastes bad, what we want is not *that*, i.e., the painful experience of taking it, but rather the goal to be achieved, the restoration of one's health.

In order to clarify the goal of our wants, the text introduces a classification of things into:

(a) good things,

(b) bad things, and

(c) things in between (μεταξύ), "which sometimes partake of the good, sometimes of the bad, sometimes of neither; such as sitting, walking, running, sailing; and such as stones, sticks, and the like."[166]

Applying the previous distinction to this classification, Socrates obtains Polus' assent to the view that in our actions we pursue the intermediates for the sake of the goods, and not the other way around. Since it has already been granted that what we want is not what we do, but that for the sake of which we do it, it follows that what we want are the good things.

This conclusion establishes a logical link between what we want (or our will) and the good. Hence, if we want to discern whether someone does or does not want to do something, we will not be able to decide, say, by observing the subjective mental states of the agent (assuming that this is feasible, at least, perhaps, for the agent herself). Only a procedure analogous to objective verification will allow us to decide the matter.

If an agent performs an action for the sake of a goal that is good for her, then we may infer that she wants that goal and, consequently, the action conducive to it. If it turns out that the goal was bad for her, then, all appearances to the contrary, we conclude that she did not want to attain that specific goal, nor did she want to perform the corresponding action, because her aim was her real good. The true good is what one really wants, as opposed to what one thinks one wants. By analogy with "the apparent good," i.e., what seems to be good, we can introduce a terminological distinction between "the apparent will" and "the real will."[167]

This distinction assumes that we can be mistaken about our own good, and this, as we have seen, is clearly borne out by the choice of words in (i). The verbal form *dokei moi*, "it seems to me," is akin to the noun *doxa*, "opinion" or "belief," and a belief can be false. Something can seem to me to be the case, but in fact not be the case. I cannot be wrong in willing what is best for me, but I can be wrong in thinking that X is best for me.

If a tyrant decides to expel a citizen or to confiscate his property, and this generates a revolt that leads to the overthrow of the tyrant, the tyrant will have done what seemed best to him, but not what he ultimately wanted.

If power is characterized as what is good for the person who wields it, and if the tyrant does things that are not good for him, it logically follows that he is not powerful, no matter how capable he is of injuring his subjects with impunity.

Accordingly, Socrates claims that he has justified his thesis that successful orators are not strong. Several objections to this conclusion can be raised. In fact, the argument really proves that orators are weak only when they make mistakes. They have power when they do not err. Indeed we can imagine an orator or a tyrant who never makes mistakes in his political calculations.[168] In the *Gorgias* this line of thought is not pursued explicitly, but the concept of the human good, which develops as the conversation moves forward, will show that orators and tyrants are *always* wrong because in their decisions they do not consider the only factor that can guarantee a good outcome for themselves.

Power, Justice, and Happiness

A new shift in the conversation is prompted by a question Polus addresses to Socrates. He suggests that, with regard to power, Socrates feels the same as everybody else:

(S40) As if you, Socrates, would not welcome the freedom to do in the city what seems [best] to you, rather than not! Are you not envious [ζηλοῖς] when you see someone killing whomever he thought [best to kill], or confiscating his property, or putting him in bonds?[169]

Polus is so convinced that power is desirable that he assumes even Socrates, in contemplating the deeds of the truly powerful, experiences jealousy, the emotion which arises when we see someone in possession of what we ourselves would like to have.

Socrates, in turn, counters with a question that baffles Polus, though the question is not surprising to the reader of the early dialogues, who will find it directly relevant to the application of principle (P3) ("Every agent, in performing an action, should consider *exclusively* whether what he is about to do is just or unjust"). The exchange that ensues provides a justification for (P3):

(S41) (= immediately following S40) Soc.: Do you mean [that he does all of that] justly or unjustly?
Pol.: Whichever way, isn't he to be envied in either case?
Soc.: Watch your words, Polus!
Pol.: Why?
Soc.: Because one should not envy the unenviable or the miserable, but rather pity them.
Pol.: What? Do you think that's the condition of the men I'm talking about?
Soc.: Of course.
Pol.: Then someone who kills whomever he thinks [best to kill], and does so justly, seems to you to be miserable and worthy of pity?
Soc.: No, not to me; but neither [does he seem to me] enviable.
Pol.: Didn't you just say he was miserable?
Soc.: [I meant] the one who kills unjustly, my friend, and worthy of pity as well, but the one who kills justly is not enviable.
Pol.: Surely the one who is killed unjustly is pitiable and miserable.
Soc.: Less so than the killer, Polus, and less so than the one who is killed justly.
Pol.: How so, Socrates?
Soc.: Because the greatest of evils [μέγιστον τῶν κακῶν, the greatest of the things that are bad for oneself] is actually to do wrong [τὸ ἀδικεῖν, to do what's unjust].
Pol.: Is *that* the greatest? Isn't to suffer wrong greater still?
Soc.: No, not at all.

Pol.: So you would want to suffer wrong rather than to do wrong?
Soc.: I wouldn't want either of them, but if I had to either do or suffer wrong, I would choose to suffer rather than to do wrong.[170]

A few lines from later in the conversation round off the sketch of Socratic ethics:

(S42) Pol.: How so? Does the whole of happiness [consist] in that [= on how one stands with respect to education and justice]?
Soc.: So indeed I say, Polus. For I hold that the noble [καλόν] and good [ἀγαθόν] man or woman is happy, whereas the unjust [ἄδικον] and wicked [πονερόν] is miserable.[171]

What insight into Socrates' views do these lines provide? Before we examine them, we should note that irony seems to have virtually disappeared, at least with regard to the claims made here. Socrates speaks quite emphatically in the first person singular ("So indeed I say," "for I hold").

In (S42) Socrates makes an assertion about the character of those who are happy. If actions are taken to determine character, then Socrates' thesis matches the following principle:

(P14) The greatest good, i.e., happiness, consists in noble and good action.

In classical Greek, the adjectives used in (S42) to identify the happy or flourishing man were often combined to form a single expression (καλὸς κἀγαθός, "noble-and-good") which was commonly applied to the perfect gentleman. This was primarily an expression used to indicate social prominence, but it also possessed a moral connotation. The context here shows that the latter meaning of the combined terms is uppermost in Socrates' mind, for he describes the individual in the state diametrically opposed to happiness—i.e., the miserable or wretched man—in strictly moral terms: the unhappy man, Socrates affirms, is the unjust and wicked one.

The same thesis had been asserted in (S41):

(P15) The greatest evil consists in unjust action.

Our interpretation of (S42), then, yields (P14), a principle equivalent to the principle found in the *Crito*, which expresses Socrates' fundamental conviction about the good for a human being: the good is the morally right.

The distinction between what an agent wants and what seems best to him provides textual evidence for a principle which should be added to our list:

(P16) Every agent wants his own real good.

This is doubtless a descriptive principle. If true, it states what agents do in fact aim at through their actions. Its primary role falls within the domain of action theory. Socrates assumes such a principle when he attempts to *explain* the actions of orators and tyrants. Alongside this, we should consider a closely related normative principle which could be formulated:

(P17) Every agent ought to want his own real good.

Since happiness or the good life embraces everything that is good for human beings, it is fair to say that we have already encountered a principle equivalent to (P17). In the *Crito*, Socrates and his friend agreed that they should value, not life, but the good life, above all else. This agreement is the textual basis for (P11). Furthermore, (P17) not only is a different formulation of (P11); it is also closely akin to our initial criterion for practical rationality: (P1): "a choice is rational if and only if it is a choice of what is best for the agent."

Given (P14) and (P15), i.e., the specification of what is ultimately good and what is ultimately bad for us, and (P1), the principle for practical rationality, we have uncovered a rigorous, deductive justification of principle (P3) ("an agent should consider *exclusively* whether her action will be just or unjust"), the decision-making principle which plays a prominent role in the *Apology*. If we ought to aim at our good (in the prudential sense of "ought") and if our good consists in morally right action (morally wrong action being bad for us), then we ought (again, prudentially speaking) to consider whether or not what we are about to do is right or wrong. This form of deliberation is indeed a necessary condition to avoid evils and secure goods.

This interpretation, I believe, confirms part of my analysis of the *Crito* in the last chapter: the structure of Socratic ethics is essentially prudential because its cornerstone is a normative principle which exhorts us to pursue our own real good.

Justifying Intellectualism

As we saw, the *Gorgias* introduces, beyond the doctrines of the *Crito*, the explanatory principle (P16). It is noteworthy that this principle also appears in a transition dialogue, namely the *Meno*.[172] According to (P17), irrationality and, by implication, morally wrong action may be due to unwillingness on the part of the agent to pursue his own good. This failure could be explained as weakness of the will. But if (P16) is true, this is impossible. If an agent always wills the good, then the explanation of wrong action has to be sought solely in the agent's failure to know what is good for him.

I am inclined to suppose that while (P17) is likely to be a genuine Socratic formulation, (P16) was introduced by Plato when he came to realize that Socratic intellectualism required a different formulation of its initial premise. Socratic intellectualism, in fact, strictly follows from assumptions which include (P16) and not (P17). The knowledge of justice which suffices to make an individual who has acquired it a just individual[173] involves two distinct components:

(i) knowledge of specific criteria for just action, and
(ii) knowledge that just action is good for the agent.

In conjunction with (P16), knowledge of (i) and (ii) entails that the individual will act justly. If he does not behave justly, and if (P16) is not challenged, then we may infer that the individual lacks (i) or (ii), or both. The kind of ignorance most directly relevant for the dramatic plot of the *Gorgias* is, of course, ignorance of (ii), i.e., of the fact that justice is in the best interest of the agent himself. The tyrant who arbitrarily kills his opponents does so unwillingly because he does not know that he is harming himself. Had he known it, he would not have committed such crimes.

The result is paradoxical, and the validity of this inference has not gone unchallenged.[174] The harshness of the paradox is due to the conflict between the ordinary use of the expressions "to do willingly," "to want," "to will" (in Greek or English) and the new use suggested by Socrates. Nevertheless, some of the assumptions leading to the paradox may well be true.

Against the thesis that human agents aim at their real good, it can be argued that in fact we see them aiming only at what appears to them to be good. But to aim at the apparent good is to aim at what one believes to be *really* good. If that belief is true, then the real and the apparent good do in fact coincide. If it is false, and the agent can be made aware of the falsehood, the real good becomes apparent to the agent and the original apparent good is taken for what it really is, i.e., bad.

The process of correcting one's beliefs about the good, however, may be arduous or virtually impossible to carry out. Deception and, most of all, deeply ingrained self-deception about what is in one's best interest are well-attested phenomena.

Perhaps the most problematic of the assumptions behind the intellectualist thesis (viz., "no one does wrong wanting to do it")[175] is the identification of the real good with the moral good. In the *Gorgias* we shall discover an attempt to prove this.

The Role of Nonmoral Goods

The clear conception of his own good leads Socrates to avow in (S41) that he would prefer to suffer an injustice rather than commit one. But he also states that he would prefer not to have to choose between those alternatives. Indeed, most of our choices are not of this nature. We can often act justly or avoid acting unjustly without much risk of being victims of injustice ourselves. Usually we face many morally legitimate options none of which amount to doing anything wrong.

Any case in which one of the options we confront does involve doing wrong (with or without the risk of suffering wrong) will be governed by (P3). But how are we to decide rationally what to do in those cases where nothing morally inappropriate is attached to any of the alternatives open to us? Since a rational decision is made by reference to the good, a theory that only envisages moral goods cannot offer a criterion with which to decide these cases.[176]

Does Socrates admit any goods apart from the moral goods? Within the context we are considering, Socrates ranks among the goods (as opposed to the bad things and those in between) a few nonmoral items: "Wisdom (*sophia*),[177] health, wealth, and the like."[178] However, we must turn to the *Euthydemus*, which probably belongs to the same group of dialogues as the *Gorgias*, to examine a passage in which the question of nonmoral goods is discussed with greater precision.

> (S43) [Soc. speaking] Well then, what are the things that are good for us? It is not difficult, nor does it require, it seems, a solemn person to answer this. For anyone would tell us that being wealthy is good. Right?
>
> Of course, he [= Clinias] said.
>
> Also being healthy and handsome, and well provided with all other [such qualities] that pertain to the body?
>
> He agreed.
>
> Moreover, are not noble birth, power, and honor in one's own [city] clearly goods?
>
> He agreed.
>
> What goods, he said, are left to us? What about being temperate and just and courageous? By Zeus, Clinias, do you think we will be right or not if we put them among the good things? Perhaps someone might dispute this. What do you think?
>
> They are goods, said Clinias.
>
> Very well, I said. And wisdom [σοφία], where shall we place it within our chorus? Among the goods? Or where would you suggest?[179]

In this scene, Socrates requests that his young companion approve a catalogue of goods which includes, in hierarchical order, material goods (wealth), physical goods (health and beauty), social goods (belonging to a noble family, different forms of power, prestige), *prima facie* moral goods (the possession of an excellence such as temperance or moderation, justice, and courage), and, finally, a good which at first glance seems to be an intellectual good (wisdom or knowledge).

Given Socrates' lack of interest in the theoretical exercise of reason and his conviction that the moral virtues are forms of knowledge,[180] it is reasonable to understand *sophia* in (S43) as excellence in the practical exercise of reason, i.e., akin to what Aristotle would later call φρόνησις, "practical wisdom," or "prudence."[181] In the *Euthydemus* the two terms appear together as synonyms. The passage following (S43) confirms this insight.[182]

What is the point of possessing the good things? If we have

them, we will fare well and be happy,[183] but possession is not enough. We have to make effective use of them.[184] That use will be adequate only under rational guidance, i.e., only if we know how to use the goods properly. Whenever this condition is not satisfied, one fails less seriously and, hence, harms oneself to a lesser degree, if one has fewer goods than if one has more.[185]

There is a difficulty in the fact that this latter rule (fewer goods, less harm) also seems to hold true for two moral virtues, viz. courage and moderation.[186] I suggest that they are included among goods which require guidance as something external to them, because the terms do not seem to refer to fully developed moral habits but rather to the natural conditions that underlie such habits. In this sense, a naturally fearless person who acts imprudently can suffer more harm than an individual who is by nature more susceptible to fear in the same circumstances.[187]

If this is correct, then Socrates' concluding reference to "all things which at the outset we said were goods"[188] includes material, physical, and social goods, as well as the natural conditions for the virtues. It is a list of all nonmoral goods. Prudence (or wisdom) and, implicitly, the moral virtues, stand apart, for prudence provides correct rational guidance and the virtues imply it. This is indeed the thesis of the paragraph which brings the argument to a close:

> (S44) [Soc. speaking] In sum, Clinias, I said, it seems [with respect to] all the things that we initially said were goods, that the account [the *logos*, the argument] was not [to the effect] that they in themselves [αὐτά γε καθ'αὐτά] are naturally good. The point, it seems, was this. If ignorance leads them, they are greater evils than their opposites, insofar as they are more capable of serving a bad leader. But if prudence and wisdom [lead them] they are greater goods, although in themselves [αὐτὰ καθ' αὐτά] neither kind is worth anything at all.[189]

In this summary, the crucial expression is doubtless *auta kath' hauta*, "[the things] according to themselves," "just by themselves." Its primary role in Greek philosophy before Socrates had been to specify something considered in isolation, i.e., apart from anything else.[190] Here it serves to draw a sharp distinction between the attributes which nonmoral goods possess in themselves and those they possess by reference to what governs their actual use. Socrates holds that, in themselves, those nonmoral items have no value; they are neither good nor bad.

But this view generates a difficulty because it seems to equate the nonmoral goods on Socrates' list in the *Euthydemus* with the "things in between" mentioned in the *Gorgias* (to sit, to walk, to run, to sail, etc. and stones, sticks, etc.).[191] In the *Gorgias*, we must recall, a few nonmoral goods were mentioned not as things "in between" but rather as generally acknowledged goods. Can the two sources be reconciled?

Perhaps a more detailed formulation of the Socratic theory of goods will suffice. (i) Things "in between" are valued, by their very nature, only as instruments, as conducive to something else. This is quite clear of sticks and stones; and if we wish to consider, e.g., sailing, we should remember that the Greeks sailed only to get to their destination. (Yachting was not a Greek sport!) (ii) Wealth, health, good looks, and similar things can doubtless be valued for their own sake. Provided they are used in conjunction with moral excellence, they cannot be said to be purely instrumental. But on the other hand, they can also be put to good or bad use. In this sense, when considered apart from the way they are used, we cannot tell whether they benefit or harm us. Therefore, we can call them "conditional goods" because they are intrinsic goods on the condition that what we do with them is morally right. They have a minor yet constitutive role to play in human well-being. (iii) Finally, at the top, there are absolute, unconditional goods, i.e., things that remain good regardless of association with anything else. These are, as we have seen, the moral goods.[192]

Can traces of this threefold classification (purely instrumental goods, conditional goods, unconditional goods) be found in the earlier dialogues, or is it a Platonic construction dating to a later period?

The *Crito* states unequivocally that the good life is the just life, a thesis affirming the overwhelming weight of the unconditional goods. An interesting reflection on illness and the value of health also appears in the *Crito*. Socrates suggests that when the body is sick, life is not worth living.[193] Health, then, seems to be highly valued. It is not a mere instrument, though it is not strictly a constitutive element of the good life. Justice with illness, or even with death, is still more desirable than injustice, however it is qualified.

What about wealth? Is it purely instrumental, or can it be considered a conditional good? There is a passage in the *Apology* that provides a lucid reply to these questions, but the Greekless reader is bound to miss it because it is usually mistranslated. One standard rendering is the following:

> "Wealth does not bring about excellence, but excellence brings about wealth and other public and private blessings for men."[194]

According to this version, Socrates exhorts people to practice moral virtue on the curious grounds that it will make them rich! If Socrates himself is virtuous and has failed to become wealthy, then he himself is the pragmatic counterexample that refutes his maxim.

Closer inspection of the Greek text reveals that the correct translation is not vulnerable to the pragmatic counterexample:

> (S45) Excellence [ἀρετή] does not come [γίγνεται, come to be] from wealth, but it is from excellence that wealth and all other things [become] goods for men, both in private and in public [life].[195]

Rendered in this way, these lines are consistent with the *Euthydemus* passage and partly confirm my formulation of the Socratic doctrine of goods. Wealth by itself does not generate excellence. Being rich does not make one honest. But honesty and justice make the possession and use of wealth a genuine good, i.e., something worth having, on the condition of prior moral excellence.

Socrates, then, seems to admit the existence of goods other than the moral goods, but assigns them a subordinate position. They do not play a role in making the crucial decisions of his life. In the choice between (a), obtaining and preserving a moral good such as justice, and (b), obtaining and preserving a nonmoral good such as wealth, health, or even one's life, the rational thing to do is to choose (a) over (b).

We can now respond to the difficulty that led us to an examination of the *Euthydemus* passage. When we confront a choice between two morally legitimate alternatives—i.e., when there is nothing morally inappropriate attached to either—how should we proceed? A simple Socratic solution would be: the rational choice is to prefer nonmoral, conditional goods over purely instrumental goods or nonmoral evils (e.g., illness, poverty). But we should remain aware of the fact that conditional goods make only a modest and almost insignificant contribution to our happiness. Assuming temperance in both cases, one should prefer a diet that leads to health rather than illness. Assuming justice, one should prefer wealth over poverty, etc. However, the good life of the virtuous man will not be seriously affected by either illness or poverty.

The existence of conditional goods explains why our texts seem to waver between passages that indicate that injustice is the *greatest* of evils (and hence that there are other evils)[196] and passages that suggest that justice is the *only* good (and hence that there are no other goods).[197] In spite of the lack of symmetry, we need not press the charge of inconsistency. The sizable disparity between the unconditional, moral goods and the conditional, nonmoral goods explains why the former, in certain contexts, may be reckoned by Socrates as virtually the only goods.

In the Introduction we suggested that there are two possible noninstrumentalist interpretations of the Socratic conception of happiness. According to the first (2a: Complete coincidence), the moral virtues are the sole constituent of happiness; according to the second (2b: Partial coincidence), happiness includes some nonmoral goods.

We are now in a position to see that the difference between these interpretations is negligible. Strictly speaking, (2b) is the correct interpretation because of the presence of conditional goods within the Socratic catalogue of goods. A morally upright person who is wealthy and healthy is (slightly) better off than someone who is not. But since the contribution of health and wealth is minimal and completely dependent on their being used in a morally correct manner, it remains true that something is good for an agent if and only if it (or its use) is morally right.[198]

The Refutation of Polus

Polus, of course, does not endorse the Socratic hierarchy of goods. On two occasions he rejects the theorem that it is better to suffer wrong than to do wrong. In his view, it is worse and more harmful to suffer it.[199] Hence, it is better to do wrong.

In response to Socrates' questions, Polus makes a concession that will lead him into insurmountable difficulties. Polus admits that although it is worse to suffer wrong, it is αἴσχιον, *aischion*, "uglier," "more shameful," to do wrong.[200]

This concession corresponds to the view, shared by most ancient Greeks, that there are rules governing life in the community and that breaking those rules, especially those that protect the rights and possessions of others, is unacceptable. Taking unfair advantage of others is frowned upon and regarded as ugly or socially unbecoming.

It should be noted that the conjunction of the two views expressed by Polus:

doing wrong is better,

and

doing wrong is more shameful,

implies an outright rejection of the Socratic doctrine that the decisive goods are the moral goods. In fact, that doctrine entails that whatever is shameful is not better but worse for the agent.[201] Hence, we are led to expect that, in refuting Polus, Socrates will indirectly offer a defense of a fundamental tenet of his moral philosophy.

Socrates' refutation of Polus tacitly assumes a strict symmetry between certain predicates and relies initially on their ordinary use. The symmetrical predicates in this case are *aischron*, an adjective whose comparative is *aischion*, and *kalon*. These predicates are taken as symmetrical in the sense that the criteria for the application of one are exactly opposite those governing application of the other.

Socrates starts the *elenchus* by getting Polus to grant that the criterion for calling something *kalon* is that the object must be either useful or pleasant to contemplate, or both. In order to understand his point (and Polus' immediate assent), one should notice that *kalon* is one of the most widely used terms of commendation in Greek.

Something can be commended as *kalon* if it is beautiful and generates enjoyment when one sees it; i.e., if it exhibits aesthetic qualities. Something can also be praised as *kalon* if it is well made and is therefore an efficient instrument. Consider a shield. If it has been well crafted, it may be *kalon*, both because of its aesthetically pleasing qualities and because of its usefulness in stopping missiles.

But there is a third use of *kalon* which was mentioned in the previous chapter. According to this use, we commend as *kalon* whatever is praiseworthy from a moral point of view.

Because of the three different ways in which the term can be employed in Greek, the rendering of *kalon* in English will vary. In some instances it can adequately be rendered by "beautiful" (in a basically aesthetic sense), in other instances by "useful," "good," or "beneficial" (in an instrumental sense akin to "apt," "efficient"), and in still others by "good" (in the moral sense, i.e., "admirable," "fine," "noble").[202] Within the argument, Socrates' strategy is to define the *moral* sense of the word by reference to its two other uses, i.e., the *aesthetic* and the *instrumental* sense, either separately or jointly.

Once Polus admits that something is *aischron* for the opposite reasons, i.e., either because of the pain it produces or because it is bad,[203] and the comparative use of both predicates is explained by reference to excess in any of the four factors involved (pleasure, benefit, pain, and badness, taken either separately or jointly), Socrates applies the definitional results to the evaluation of doing versus suffering wrong.

If doing something unjust is *aischion*, then it will surpass doing something just either in pain or in badness, or both. It is clear that doing wrong is not more painful than suffering wrong. On the contrary, the victim is the one who undergoes more pain (e.g., being tortured, or being arrested and sent into exile). It follows that doing wrong will be *aischion* on the grounds specified by the other term of the disjunction that defines the shameful: its badness. Therefore, Socrates concludes, since it is not more painful, then it is worse to do wrong than to suffer wrong.

Is this argument persuasive? Scholars have called attention to two kinds of difficulties that cast doubts on its validity.

In the argument, there are several substitutions of terms which amount to transitions from one notion to a slightly different one. To go from "useful" to "(instrumentally) good" is probably legitimate, but to move from "painful to see" (a reasonable substitution for "ugly," the term opposed to "pleasant to see") to "painful (without qualification)" is hardly acceptable. Indeed, it is doubtful that *aischron* can ever have this meaning (*lyperon* is the most common term for "painful"); and if the standard meaning ("ugly") is retained, it can be argued that the contemplation of an act of injustice is in fact painful for the observer. The greater or lesser pain is allotted not to either one of the participants (the person who does wrong or the one who suffers wrong), but to a third party. This, I believe, is implied in Polus' key admission. Acts of injustice are socially painful. If this is the case, it simply does not follow that doing wrong is worse.[204]

The second difficulty is whether it is legitimate to explain the moral use of a term by reducing it to its aesthetic or its instrumental use, or both. I am inclined to respond in the negative, because there are no conceptual links between the pleasant and the morally right, as Socrates will show in his discussion with Callicles. Nor are there any conceptual links between what is beneficial for a person and what it would be right for that person to do; i.e., between standard uses of "(instrumentally) good" and "right." Most speakers of Greek or English would grant that these two predicates mean something different and unrelated. One cannot be defined or explained through the other. As we have seen, the identification of the good (albeit, the noninstrumental good) and the right is a substantive thesis of Socratic ethics and not a statement about the ordinary meaning of the words.

It would be odd, therefore, to hold that the definition of *kalon* that is operative in the argument corresponds to Socrates' own view. The definition is clearly intended as an *ad hominem* move. Socrates offers Polus a chance to express what is probably a well-ingrained conviction in the mind of the young Sicilian: that the admirable things are those that give us pleasure or are to our benefit.[205]

The argument then does not make a direct contribution to the justification of the Socratic thesis. In a way, it begs the question by assuming, definitionally, that if something morally commendable is not pleasant, it will have to be, by the very meaning of the term, beneficial.

The net result of the discussion with Polus shows that a position which views unbridled political power as most choiceworthy, and at the same time accepts a negative moral judgment about certain uses of that power, is an incoherent position. The incoherence lies in the fact that power is considered to be both unconditionally good and at the same time bad under certain conditions. Polus fails to provide an adequate alternative to the moral ideas of Socrates.

A well-rounded interpretation of the confrontation with Polus would now require an exposition of the theory of punishment that supplements it.[206] I do not think, however, that this is necessary for our purposes, because I fail to see any new elements of Socrates' moral philosophy disclosed in the corresponding section of the text. The major paradox in it ("if one has done wrong, then it is better to be punished than to escape scot free") is a direct corollary of the thesis that moral transgressions are the worst evils. Punishment, like purgative medicine, is the appropriate instrument to rid oneself of such evils.

In the discussion with Callicles we shall find new developments affecting the core of the Socratic position.

Before moving on, however, we should note that, consistent with the *Apology* and the *Crito*, there is thus far no direct attempt on the part of Socrates to justify the principles of his moral philosophy. Those principles are only indirectly validated *vis-à-vis* the interlocutor, who finally accepts them after his initial position has been refuted. In this sense, it can be claimed that there is no attempt at justification beyond the boundaries of the dialogue itself. The refutation starts from an agreement (or the tacit assumption of one) within the conversation, and this agreement expresses a commonly held view (e.g., that one ought to remain where one's commander has ordered one to stay; that fair agreements ought to be honored; that it is more shameful to do than to suffer wrong). No further reasons are given to urge their acceptance. The crucial thing is that the interlocutor accept them.[207]

In the confrontation with Callicles, this trait of the *elenchus* is retained, but a new kind of justification is introduced to persuade the reader of the truth of the basic moral propositions.

V

Callicles and the Platonic Justification of Socratic Ethics

Callicles' main line of attack on Socratic ethics relies on a distinction that has been traced back to the Sophistic movement, viz. the distinction between *physis* ("nature") and *nomos* ("custom," "law," "convention").[208] Callicles understands this distinction as marking a contrast between that which is given or born without human intervention and that which results from human agreements. *Physis* possesses an objective, solid reality; *nomos* depends on the subjective opinions and choices of men. In Callicles' view, the natural and the customary are not at the same level. The natural is the superior reality; human customs are vastly inferior.[209]

Callicles' defense of the superiority of nature is a remarkable piece of moral reasoning that deserves to be quoted *verbatim*:

> (S46) Socrates, in your speeches you seem to behave with youthful insolence, acting like a true demagogue. You are doing this now that Polus has had the same thing done to him that he accused you of inflicting on Gorgias. Polus said, you see, that when you asked Gorgias whether he would teach a student who came to him wishing to study rhetoric, but not knowing the just [τὰ δίκαια, the just things], Gorgias was ashamed and replied he would teach [it to] him. He did this because men are usually vexed if someone refuses. And because of this admission, he [= Polus] added, Gorgias was forced to contradict himself, and that is precisely what you like. Polus laughed at you at the time, and rightly so, in my opinion. But now exactly the same thing has happened to him. *I* do not admire Polus for that very reason: he agreed with you that to do wrong is more shameful than to suffer wrong. As a result of this admission, he was bound and muzzled by you in the discussion, being ashamed to say what he thought.

In fact, Socrates, while claiming to pursue the truth, you lead [the discussion] to the vulgarities of demagogues which are not admirable by nature [φύσει], but are so [only] by custom [νόμῳ, by social agreement, by law]. For the most part, these two, nature and custom, are opposed to each other, so that if someone is ashamed and does not dare to say what he thinks, he is compelled to contradict himself. This is the clever trick you have grasped which enables you to make mischief in your conversations. If someone speaks according to custom, you slyly question him according to nature; if [he speaks of] the natural [τὰ τῆς φύσεως, "the things of nature"], [you ask him about] the customary [τὰ τοῦ νόμου, the things of custom, what the law prescribes].

That is just what happened in our discussion of doing wrong versus suffering wrong. When Polus mentioned what is more shameful according to custom, you pursued the argument according to nature. For by nature everything is more shameful which is also worse, [e.g.] suffering wrong, whereas by custom it is [more shameful] to do wrong. It does not befit a man to undergo the suffering of injustice. It befits a slave for whom it would be better to die than to live, because, if he is wronged and abused, he cannot defend himself or anyone else he cares about.

I believe that those who enact the laws [νόμοι, customs][210] are the weak men, i.e., the many. It is for themselves and their own advantage that they enact the laws and assign praise or blame. They frighten the stronger men, those who are capable of having more [πλέον ἔχειν], and in order to prevent them [= the strong] from having more than they themselves, they [= the many] state that overreaching others [πλεονεκτεῖν] is shameful and wrong, and that doing wrong consists in this, attempting to have more than other people. I believe they are delighted if they themselves get an equal share [τὸ ἴσον] because they are inferior. These are the reasons why to attempt to have more than the many is said to be wrong and shameful by custom, and why they call it doing wrong.

But I believe nature itself makes it clear that it is right [δίκαιον, just] for the better to have more than the worse, the stronger than the weaker. [Nature] shows that this is the case in many areas, not only among the other animals but also in entire cities and races of men, where the right [τὸ δίκαιον, justice] has been judged to consist in the superior ruling the inferior and having more than he. For what kind of right did Xerxes rely on when he campaigned against Greece? Or his father [Darius] against the Scythians?[211] Countless examples of the same sort could be mentioned. I believe these men do those things in accordance with the nature of the right [of the just, of justice]—yes, by Zeus, in accordance with the custom [law] of nature, though not perhaps in accordance with the custom [law] we lay down. We mold the best and strongest among ourselves, catching them young, like lion cubs; and with charms and incantations we enslave them, telling them that they ought to have equal shares [τὸ ἴσον, the equal], and that this is the admirable and the right [τὸ δίκαιον, the just, justice]. But I believe that if a man is born with a strong enough nature, he will shake off, tear apart, and escape all this. He will trample upon our writings [= written statutes?], our spells and our charms, and all the laws contrary to nature. This slave of ours will rise up and reveal himself our master [δεσπότης], and the justice of nature will then suddenly burst into light.[212]

Callicles' speech does not stop here, but with this reference to an almost mystical manifestation of natural justice, he reaches the climax of his impassionate intervention.

Callicles' initial thesis is that Socrates is aware of the *nomos-physis* distinction, and that he makes fraudulent use of it in his conversations. The claim is that Socrates, unbeknownst to his interlocutor, introduces semantic variations in his use of the fundamental moral and evaluative predicates.

According to Callicles, Socrates applies the predicate *aischion* ("more shameful," "uglier") to the act of committing an injustice, and he does so in the customary or conventional sense of this term. This is objectionable because, in Callicles' view, the terms that should govern the discussion are the predicates "good" and "bad" in their natural sense.

Being a victim of injustice, being harmed and abused without being able to defend oneself or one's friends, those are the naturally bad things and *therefore*, according to Callicles, the naturally shameful ones. Weakness leads to shame. The good and the admirable, by contrast, consist in being strong enough to have it one's own way and not be subject to mistreatment by others. The paradigmatic consequence of strength is labeled by Callicles *pleonexia*, using a noun derived from *pleon echein*, "to possess more." The term designates a drive toward unequal and unfair acquisition of wealth and power, the sort of ambition that Greek democratic ideology sought to restrain. Indeed, *to ison*, "the equal," "equality," in this passage stands for the slogan of democracy.[213] But for Callicles, democratic egalitarianism is despicable: he thinks natural justice will shine only if a strong man imposes his will on the city as *despotes*, i.e., as a tyrant.[214]

According to Callicles, Polus made the mistake of granting that actively committing injustice is more shameful by nature, when in fact it is only shameful by custom or social convention. The truly shameful thing, as we have seen, is to be the victim, because it is the worst thing that can happen to a man.

What is, in Callicles' opinion, the best thing that can happen to a man? We are offered a reply when Callicles supplements his earlier views by giving a specific content to his concept of the ultimate human goal. According to Callicles, wealth—but above all, political power[215]—plays a decisive role in securing what he calls "the right life,"[216] "excellence and happiness."[217] Living rightly, he holds, consists in letting one's appetites (*epithymiai*) grow as large as possible and then satisfying them.[218]

In present-day terminology we would say that Callicles defends a radical form of hedonistic egoism according to which the greatest amount of prospective pleasure for oneself counts as the ultimate criterion for making one's decisions. My pleasure not only is good; it is my sole good.

Living rightly in Callicles' sense means satisfying the requirements of natural morality (*to kata physin kalon kai dikaion*, "the admirable and just according to nature").[219] The ethics of moderation (*sophrosyne*, "self-control") and of respect for the rights of others (*dikaiosyne*, "justice")[220] is simply "contrary to nature" (*para physin*).[221]

Since Socrates is surely an upholder of the sort of ethics envisioned here, it seems reasonable to suppose that, either during his lifetime or shortly thereafter, individuals familiar with the nature/convention distinction may have raised the objection that Socrates' principles were simply the result of an agreement between participants in a conversation (and thus true by convention), without any grounding in the nature of things. If only the norms based on *physis* were objectively valid, whereas those which merely constituted *nomos* embodied the interests of the group that laid them down, then Socrates' moral philosophy would be highly suspect.

These considerations lead us to ask whether Socrates did attempt to find a "natural" foundation or justification for the starting points of his ethics. This point has considerable interest, because if he did, Socrates would be the initiator of a long tradition in Western thought known as the natural law position in moral philosophy.[222] It is surely ironic for Plato to let Callicles coin the expression ὁ νόμος τῆς φύσεως, "the custom [or law] of nature," thus combining two things Callicles sees as radically opposed. Callicles' natural law, of course, amounts to the thesis that the habitual behavior of animals and men in the natural world shows that such behavior is justified. The natural exercise of power manifests that there is a right to such exercise; in short, that might implies right.[223] Needless to say, this is exactly the opposite of the claims made by later theories of natural law.[224]

If we search the early dialogues for awareness of the desirability of a natural foundation for ethics, we initially find the use of what may be called "natural analogies." In the *Crito*, for example, the reason to disregard the moral opinion of the majority is that one should not accept their opinion in matters pertaining to the well-being of the body.[225] The many are not qualified physicians. By analogy, when we make a decision, we should consider how it will affect the well-being or good of the soul, and the many are not experts in this domain either. According to Socrates, the well-being of the soul is defined exclusively in moral terms. There is no reference to an optimal state of the soul which could be described in purely nonmoral terms because there are no nonmoral properties which make a soul a good soul. Socrates does not seem to envision in the *Crito* a state of the soul which could yield a "natural" premise for ethics.

Perhaps a more promising strategy in the search for natural foundations for ethics would be to assume that things have a central core or nature which manifests itself in certain recurring patterns of behavior. Those invariable tendencies may be taken to display what nature itself requires from things of that sort. I think it is fair to say that this is very much Callicles' strategy in his effort to refute the Socratic position. Callicles invokes the observable fact that human beings have a natural tendency to acquire more and more wealth and power. *Pleonexia*, the drive to possess more than others, is a genuine manifestation of their nature. Hence, he seems to conclude, actions in accordance with this drive are perfectly licit.

How does Socrates react to this doctrine which claims to be firmly grounded on the requirements of nature?

Socrates and the Nature-Convention Distinction

Socrates can choose either one of two ways to respond to the challenge. The first alternative is simply to declare that any reference to nature and its alleged manifestations is strictly irrelevant to ethical thought. Accordingly, the natural human inclination to pursue pleasure, power, and wealth would not justify those acts conforming to its impulses, or those opposing them. On this view there would be no such thing as a "natural foundation of ethics."

The second alternative consists in arguing for a reinterpretation of the concept of nature so that not everything that happens to be the case, no matter how frequently it takes place, is considered natural. This requires a clear distinction between a descriptive concept of nature and a normative one. Only the latter would allow us to discern whether a given inclination or behavior is justifiable.

In the *Gorgias*, Socrates pursues a strategy closer to the second alternative, but he does so while avoiding explicit mention of the term *physis*. In opposition to Callicles, who insists on letting actions be governed by what appears to be natural, Socrates reiterates the thesis that our actions should take the good as their ultimate reference point. In the development of his argument, however, an important connection is established between the notion of the good and the structure of the natural world.

But before we turn to the argument that establishes that connection (and to the rejection of hedonism), we should take note of the only argument in which Socrates explicitly uses the Greek term for nature, which appears before Callicles formulates his hedonistic position. The steps of this *ad hominem* piece of reasoning may be loosely paraphrased as follows:[226]

(i) By nature, the strong man has a right to dominate the weak (Callicles' thesis).

(ii) By nature, the many are stronger than a singular individual (granted by Callicles).

(iii) By nature, the many have a right to dominate the strong man [from (i) and (ii)].

(iv) By nature, the many have a right to enact the egalitarian conventions [from (iii)].

(v) Egalitarian conventions determine that to do wrong is more shameful than to suffer wrong and that equal shares is the just (asserted by Callicles).

(vi) By nature and not only by convention, to do wrong is more shameful than to suffer wrong, and equal shares is the just [from (iv) and (v)].

In order to avoid the rejection of his position entailed by (vi), Callicles rejects premise (ii) by modifying his interpretation of "strong man": to be strong is not merely to have physical strength, and hence to be at the mercy of the physically stronger crowd; it consists in being politically astute as well and capable of attaining one's goals.[227] Having these qualities amounts to being intelligent (*phronimos*, practically wise, prudent) and courageous (*andreios*, brave, manly). Though these attributes are commonly used to bestow socially acceptable praise on an individual, Callicles understands them in a nonstandard way: prudence, he believes, is a certain shrewdness to understand the workings of power, and courage is nothing but a form of ruthlessness.

Instead of recasting his argument to make it work now that one of its key terms ("the strong man") has been redefined, Socrates seizes the opportunity to redirect the conversation toward moderation and justice, the other two canonical excellences. Does the man who has the right to rule others rule himself?[228] Does he, that is, possess *sophrosyne* (self-control, moderation, temperance, chastity)?

Callicles reacts angrily to this suggestion and, in opposition to it, formulates the extreme hedonistic thesis which, as we saw, caps his conception of natural morality. Self-control, the disposition to renounce pleasure when it is inappropriate to pursue it, is in his view sheer stupidity and a form of slavery. Justice, as conventionally understood, is the lack of courage to take for oneself what is not one's own. It is the weak man's virtue.

Socrates does not seem to be affected by the claim that self-control, justice, and similar things are "unnatural compacts of men" (παρὰ φύσιν συνθήματα ἀνθρώπων),[229] nor by the suggestion that hedonism accords with nature. He does not deal with such foundational issues directly, but proceeds to advance arguments showing that the hedonistic thesis is itself false, regardless of its relation to nature.[230]

Hedonism Rejected

The *Gorgias* offers three successive antihedonistic arguments. We shall examine them in their essentials.[231]

The first argument extends from 494b 7 to 495c 2. Its structure is relatively simple and easy to grasp, but it is fair to say that its actual force has been rediscovered only recently, as we shall see.

First, Socrates mentions certain pleasures (eating when one is hungry and drinking when one is thirsty) which Callicles readily endorses as conducive to the happy life. Socrates then mentions scratching when one itches and asks whether scratching one's whole life long is also similarly conducive to happiness. Callicles finds the idea absurd, but grants the point.

Socrates asks next about scratching one's head only when it itches and about further scratching to satisfy an itch, thus arriving at what he views as the ultimate example of "scratching": the life of the *kinaidoi* (this term refers to individuals who engage in a particular kind of sexual activity, which I shall discuss shortly in more detail). Callicles reacts with indignation and finds it shameful for Socrates to lead the discussion to such topics. Callicles admits that consistency requires him to grant that if pleasure is the same as the good, then any instance of pleasure, without restriction, will be good, even the one that has now aroused his indignation. Socrates at this point questions the sincerity of Callicles' concessions.

It is quite clear that the key to understanding the argument lies with the interpretation of the term *kinaidos*. Until recently there was considerable uncertainty as to the exact sense of this word, usually translated as "catamite" (a word derived from "Ganymede," the name of a boy whom Zeus loved and made his cup-bearer). A common assumption was that "the life of catamites" designated, rather vaguely, "a life of extreme sexual debauchery,"[232] but after the publication of K. Dover's important book on Greek homosexuality, we are in a better position to understand more precisely the import of this expression.[233] Apparently, a *kinaidos* is either a man who practices homosexual prostitution or one who acquiesces to certain submissive kinds of treatment on the part of his lover, e.g., who submits to anal coitus. In this latter case, he is called *kinaidos*, even if he does not receive payment for his services. At any rate, it seems that in Athens the second kind of activity was assimilated to the first and that both were severely punished. The penalty included loss of political rights and even the death penalty if the convicted man attempted to address the Assembly.[234] Leading the life of *kinaidoi* means, therefore, running the risk of being excluded from politics, and hence from attaining power.

The force of the *ad hominem* argument lies then in the fact that Socrates offers Callicles an example of a life devoted to pleasure, which is radically incompatible with Callicles' own ideals of manliness and unlimited political power. Nevertheless, in order to avoid inconsistency in his position, Callicles continues to maintain that pleasure and the good are the same.

After a brief interlude, Socrates proceeds to display a second argument (495e–497d). Its structure is common to many proofs of nonidentity: it is first shown that a given object has a property *P* and then that an object which seems to be identical with it does not have this property. The conclusion is that we have two objects and not just one. If you and I are talking about Mary, but the person you have in mind is blonde whereas the one I am referring to is not, then it turns out that we are talking about two different persons.

The proof in the text does not consider single objects, but pairs (good/bad, pleasure/pain). The first pair has the property of excluding each other. A good such as health does not occur concurrently with the opposite evil, sickness, in the same part of the body, e.g. the eyes. When the eyes get rid of the illness called *ophthalmia*, health does not also cease. On the contrary. It is precisely at this moment that the eyes acquire health. The same holds for other pairs of goods/evils, in particular for happiness and its opposite, misery. They are all mutually exclusive states. They are acquired and lost in succession, not concurrently.

Pain and pleasure do not behave in the same way. It is pleasant to have a drink only when one is undergoing, at the same time, the pain called "thirst." The pleasures of eating and drinking, in fact, presuppose simultaneous painful states—e.g., hunger and thirst—if they are to occur. Those pleasures also cease when the corresponding pain vanishes. Since this does not hold for the pair good/evil, it follows that the pleasant and the good (as well as the painful and the bad) are not identical.

Various difficulties arise with this argument. It can be countered that not all pleasures presuppose pain (e.g., aesthetic and intellectual pleasures do not), but this is not decisive, because the argument only requires Socrates to show that at least *some* pleasures are not good. Any difference between a pleasure and a good will show them to be nonidentical.

Also, an objection can be made that, in the case of eating and drinking, the pain of need and the pleasure of its satisfaction may not be strictly simultaneous, a point admitted in the *Phaedo*. The simultaneity claim is dropped in that dialogue and is replaced by the claim that the pain of need and the pleasure of satisfaction are nevertheless necessarily tied to each other.[235] Even if we grant that simultaneity is inadequate for describing this phenomenon, the second argument is successful in showing a significant difference between the two pairs. Certain forms of pleasure and the antecedent pains that function as a necessary condition for their occurrence are linked in a way that is not found in the mutually exclusive pair good and bad.

The third argument (497e–499b) has a similar structure, but it is formulated in terms that are far more disturbing for Callicles.

At the outset, it is granted that the presence of something good, e.g. courage, is responsible for an individual's being good, e.g. courageous. Socrates then adds that Callicles' identification of pleasure and the good warrants a substitution that yields the claim that the presence of pleasure (= good) is responsible for an individual's being good or even excellent in the sense introduced by Callicles himself, i.e., politically shrewd and ruthless.

The remaining questions aim at extracting from Callicles some concessions with regard to emotions felt on the battlefield. When the enemy is seen approaching, both the courageous and the cowardly soldiers feel pain, but perhaps the cowards feel more of it. When the enemy withdraws, both feel joy, but the cowards maybe more so. Hence, since the presence of pleasure determines goodness (= Callicles' intelligence and courage), the courageous and the cowardly will be equally good, and in many cases the cowards will be better than the courageous.

The absurdity of the conclusion finally forces Callicles to concede that some pleasures are better than others, and that some are worse. Pleasure and pain are subjective feelings that anyone can experience and hence do not furnish criteria to judge goodness and badness. Human excellence or virtue must consist in something else.

The Argument from Goodness as Order

Once Callicles' hedonism and its alleged naturalism have been shown to be inconsistent with his own conception of human excellence, Socrates develops a positive argument in defense of his own position. Its key notions are derived by analogy from the crafts or *technai* in the following section of the dialogue:

> (S47) Soc.: . . . just like all the other craftsmen, each of whom keeps his own work [ἔργον, product] in view, and does not select and add at random what he adds to it, but so that his work may acquire a certain form [εἶδος, shape]. If you wish, take a look, for example, at painters, builders, shipwrights, and all other craftsmen—whichever one you want—and see how each of them places whatever he places in a certain arrangement [τάξις, disposition, position, order], and forces one thing to fit and harmonize with another until the thing becomes a systematically arranged [τεταγμένον, from *taxis*] and ordered [κεκοσμημένον, from *kosmos*] whole. Likewise, the other craftsmen we just mentioned, the ones that deal with the body, [e.g.] physical trainers and physicians, impart order [κοσμοῦσι, from *kosmos*] and [a systematic] arrangement [συντάττουσιν, from *syn* and *taxis*]. Do we agree that this is so, or not?
> Cal.: Let it be so.
> Soc.: So if a house attains arrangement and order, it will be a good one; if it is in disarray, it will be a wretched one?
> Cal.: I agree.
> Soc.: And the same holds for a ship?
> Cal.: Yes.
> Soc.: And surely for our bodies too?
> Cal.: Certainly.
> Soc.: What about the soul? Will it be a good one if it is in disarray, or only if it attains a certain arrangement and order?
> Cal.: Given [what we have agreed on] before, we must agree on this too.[236]

The inference in this passage seems to involve the following steps:

(1) A craft product or artificial object is good if and only if it has a certain order [*taxis* and *kosmos*].[237]

(2) A human body is good [= is in good shape, is healthy] if and only if it has a certain order.

Hence,

(3) A human soul is good [= is in good shape or disposition] if and only if it has a certain order.

This argument will be persuasive only if it is supplemented in two ways. First, a more precise notion of the order proper to the soul is needed. As long as this is not supplied, the conclusion fails to have enough content to have action-guiding force for someone who might accept it as true. Second, (3) will be acceptable only if it is the conclusion of a valid and sound argument. This requires a general principle which, if true, will make it impossible for (3) to be false.

The text of the *Gorgias* provides both supplements. Socrates introduces the specification of the order of the soul by analogy with the body in the following passage:

> (S48) Soc.: . . . It seems to me that the name of the arrangement [τάξεσι in the plural] of the body is "healthy." From this comes health and every other bodily excellence.
> Cal.: Yes.
> Soc.: [And the name] of the arrangement and order [both in the plural] of the soul is "lawful" [νόμιμον, in accordance with *nomos*] and "law" [νόμος, custom], whence [men] become law-abiding and orderly, and these are justice and self-control.[238]

This passage is difficult because of the occurrence of the noun *nomos* where the analogy leads us to expect a descriptive adjective to be applied to instances of order present in a soul. I am inclined to believe, therefore, that *nomos* here is most likely a textual error and that we should assume that the original had instead *kosmion*, "orderly." [239]

With some trepidation about how the Greek should read, I would paraphrase the passage as follows: we apply the predicate "healthy" to the different orders of the body, in the sense that we call "healthy" any organ which contains no disorder and has all its parts in their proper disposition. From this arrangement arises health, strength, beauty, etc.; i.e., all the qualities that we attribute to a body whose organs work properly. Health is a product of healthy—i.e., well-ordered—bodily parts.

Something similar holds for the soul. We apply the predicates "law-abiding" and "orderly" to the orders of the soul, i.e., to the

different kinds of inner disposition reflected in actions performed
in accordance with the law of the community and assigning to
passions and impulses their proper place. It is because of these
dispositions that individuals become law-abiding and orderly,
and this constitutes justice and self-control. These virtues, then,
are the result of appropriate dispositions in the souls of human
agents.

The order peculiar to the soul is not directly observable, but it
can be inferred from the exercise of justice and moderation, the
same virtues that Callicles had originally rejected. However, the
decisive evaluation of these virtues is not yet complete, because
our judgment of their goodness depends on the validity of the
inference that human goodness consists in the possession of the
proper order of the human soul.

The last step we require appears in a section of the text where
the main ingredients in the refutation of Callicles are summarized.
Callicles is no longer willing to reply and Socrates is forced to provide the answers himself:

> (S49a) Soc.: Listen, then, as I recapitulate the argument from the
> beginning. Are the pleasant and the good the same?—They are not
> the same, as Callicles and I have agreed.—Should the pleasant be
> done for the sake of the good or the good for the sake of the pleas-
> ant?—The pleasant for the sake of the good.—And the pleasant is
> that by which, when it comes to be present [in us], we are pleased;
> the good that by which, when present in us, we are good?—Cer-
> tainly.—Indeed, we are good, both we and everything else which is
> good, when some excellence has come to be present [in us]?—I think
> it is necessarily so, Callicles.—But now, the excellence of each thing,
> whether of an artifact or a body—or, further, of a soul or a whole
> animal—is not best produced at random, but is due to arrangement,
> correctness and craft, the one assigned to each of them. Isn't it so?—
> I hold that it is.—So it is due to [an] arrangement that the excellence
> of each thing is something arranged and ordered.—I would say it
> is.—Therefore, a certain order, the one proper for a thing, when it
> comes to be present in the thing, makes each thing [ἕκαστον τῶν
> ὄντων, each being] good?—It seems to me so.[240]

The idea that things are good, that they have commendable
qualities when they are in possession of the order which is peculiar to each of them, is not new. The novelty in this passage is the
step toward a broader level of generality. A thesis that was ini-

tially restricted to the domain of craft products, bodies, and souls is now extended to "each being," i.e., to everything that is. Today logicians would call this a step of universal generalization.

Should the universal generalization be taken seriously, or is it merely rhetorical amplification? A prospective examination of a later passage will show, I think, that the first option is the correct one:

> (S50) For such a man [i.e., the one who does not control his appe-
> tites] would not be dear to [προσφιλής, a friend to] another human
> being, nor to a god, for he is incapable of community. And where
> there is no community [κοινωνία], there cannot be friendship
> [φιλία]. The wise men hold, Callicles, that heaven and earth, gods
> and men are held together by community and friendship, by order-
> liness, self-control, and justice. That is why they call this universe
> *kosmos* [world order], my friend, and not disorder, nor licentious-
> ness. You seem to me not to pay attention to these things, though
> you are also wise in these matters. You have failed to notice that
> geometrical equality [= equality of proportion][241] has great power
> among gods and men, but you think you should practice taking
> more [than your share, πλεονεξία] because you neglect geometry.[242]

The notion of order is not restricted here to a subset of reality. On the contrary, it is so wide that it can be applied to the whole universe. We should, therefore, take the end of (S49a) to express a universal principle which could be formulated as follows:

> (P18) A being is good if and only if it has the order proper for it.

This principle brings to a close the foundational argument summarized in (S49a). That passage continues:

> (S49b) Then a soul which has the order proper for it is better than a
> disordered one?—Necessarily so.—But the one that has order is
> orderly?—How could it not be [orderly]?—And the orderly soul is
> self-controlled?—Most necessarily.—Hence, the self-controlled
> soul is good.[243]

The complete argument now looks roughly like this:
(a) A being is good if and only if it has its proper order.
This is equivalent to (P18), a universal principle expressing a criterion for evaluating any kind of thing. Each particular thing

can be measured by reference to an inner order peculiar to things of its class, which, in the case of the products of human choice, it may or may not have. The principle does not specify, of course, what that order is. It will vary widely from one set of things to the next, and its discovery may be an arduous task. From the analogy with the crafts we can gather that there will be a close connection between the order and the specific use or activity of a thing; e.g., the order of a ship is determined by the fact that it is expected to sail appropriately; the order of a house is determined by the fact that human beings are expected to dwell comfortably in it; etc.

Furthermore, (S50) suggests that the internal order of each thing is the cause of the order that obtains among things in the universe as a whole. Natural things in heaven and earth cannot fail to possess their inner order, and this accounts for the harmony among them. Hence, the universe itself can be conceived as identical with the overarching order. The universe is a *kosmos,* and therefore good.

In its application both to the universe and to particular beings, "good" is a strictly nonmoral predicate.

(b) A human soul is good if and only if it has its proper order.

This follows from (a) because human souls are simply a subset of beings. Human souls are not an exception to the principle that the good quality of something is a function of its possessing the order proper for it.

(c) The order proper for souls is self-control (*sophrosyne,* temperance, moderation).

This is an independent premise. In support of it, the text provides first the analogy contained in (S48), which to some extent relies on linguistic affinities between the key terms. To a speaker of Greek, it seems obvious that to possess internal *kosmos* is to be *kosmios,* "orderly." But the adjective *kosmios* has moral connotations which become clear when we note that licentiousness, wantonness, unruliness, etc. are considered to be instances of lack of order, of *akosmia.*[244]

But the crucial support for (c) is to be found in (S50). The lack of moderation or self-control which manifests itself in behavior contrary to the *nomimon,* "the lawful"—i.e., contrary to the norms of communal life—makes an individual obnoxious and impossible to consort with. And life in common is a necessary condition for the higher form of harmony called "friendship." Therefore, self-control is for humans the inner order that sustains the broader human order within which it is worthwhile to live.

Indeed, the procedure to discover the proper order for a soul is analogous to the discovery of order in ships: if one sees a ship sailing well, one can conclude that it possesses order and then ascertain that order by observation. If one sees a human being living successfully within his community, one can assume that there is inner order in his soul. On closer inspection, the observance of the rules of the community show that self-control and moderation constitute that order.

Premise (c) then asserts that the general, nonmoral concept of inner order is instanciated in the case of the human soul by the moral concept of self-control.

Hence,

(d) A human soul will be good if and only if it has self-control or *sophrosyne*.

This conclusion is limited to the human soul and to only one of its virtues. The text immediately equates the self-controlled soul with the self-controlled man (as I have been doing here) and proceeds to argue that the possession of self-control entails the possession of the rest of the cardinal virtues, including courage, a virtue that Callicles conceives as opposed to self-control:

(S51) Soc.: I hold that, if the self-controlled [σώφρων, moderate] soul is good, then the soul in the opposite condition to the self-controlled one is bad. And this, we saw, is the foolish and licentious soul.— Indeed.—Moreover, wouldn't the self-controlled man do what is appropriate [τὰ προσήκοντα, the fitting things] with regard to both gods and men, for he would not be in control of himself if he did inappropriate things?—This will be necessarily so.—Surely, by doing what is appropriate with regard to human beings, he would be doing just deeds, and by doing them with regard to the gods, he would be doing pious ones. And the man who does just and pious deeds is necessarily just and pious.—That is true.—And, further, he must also be courageous, for it is not typical of a self-controlled man to pursue or avoid inappropriate things, but to pursue or avoid what he should, be it things or men, pleasures or pains, and to remain steadfast and endure where he should. Hence, it is absolutely necessary, Callicles, for the self-controlled man, since he is also just, courageous, and pious, to be a completely good man; and for the good man to do well and admirably whatever he does; and for the man who does well to be blessed and happy, while the bad man, the one who does badly, will be miserable. This would be the man in the opposite condition to that of the self-controlled. He is the licentious man, the man you were praising.[245]

The point of this passage is to display the Socratic doctrine of the unity of the virtues by showing that the possession of the basic virtues can be derived from the possession of one of them, namely *sophrosyne*.[246] Since its chief characteristic is the control of impulses and passions, it follows that whoever has this virtue will not yield to an impulse to do something impious (e.g., to steal treasures from a sanctuary) or unjust (e.g., to keep for himself a deposit entrusted to him by a neighbor). He will also check the impulse to flee in the presence of the enemy, holding his position instead. Thus, self-control also makes him brave. Finally, since *sophrosyne* entails the rest of the virtues, it follows that the self-controlled man will be the perfectly good man.

Strictly speaking, the premises from which this last conclusion has been inferred require us to take "perfectly good" as short for "having all the moral virtues," i.e., in the moral sense of the term "good"; but the text also makes provisions for the step toward goodness in the nonmoral sense. This is achieved by introducing at the end of (S51) a reference to the best possible state for a human being, viz. happiness. The best knife is the sharpest knife; likewise, the best human being, the happy or flourishing human being, is the most virtuous human being. We are therefore entitled to add a further step to the foundational reasoning we have been trying to reconstruct:

(e) A human being will be good if and only if he/she possesses the moral virtues.

According to the principle that the presence of something good makes us good,[247] it follows from (e) that the moral virtues are indeed the basic human goods, i.e., those things the possession of which make us good. If we further assume (P2) ("For every human being it is good to be a good human being"), then (e) turns out to be equivalent to the Socratic principle (P13) ("Something is good for an agent if and only if it is morally right," i.e., if it is itself an instance of morally virtuous behavior or is something obtained and used in accordance with a moral virtue). But if this equivalence obtains, it follows that a basic Socratic principle has been derived from a more general principle, viz. (P18), in conjunction with a specific interpretation of the notion of *sophrosyne*.

A metaphysical justification has therefore been offered for the most counterintuitive axiom of Socratic ethics, i.e., for (P13), thus supplying the kind of foundation necessary to rebut the charge of conventionalism. We should now raise the question of the authorship of this foundational move.

Socrates or Plato?

Insofar as we are attempting to study the history of Greek ethics, we should ask whether we can attribute to Socrates the discovery and adoption of (P18), the principle that attributes the goodness of any being to its possessing a certain order.[248] As the title of this chapter suggests, I am inclined to think not. Rather, I submit that it is a principle introduced by Plato to counter the objection that Socratic ethics lacks a nonconventional foundation.

The reasons that can be adduced for this position are roughly the following. In the first place, it is reasonable to hold that (P18) is a metaphysical principle in the Aristotelian sense. Indeed, it purports to be a true universal assertion about any being. Its claim is not restricted to a subset of the things that are; hence it is a claim about beings *qua* beings,[249] about things that are, no matter what they are. But putting forward views of this kind presupposes strong theoretical interests in a domain much broader than the domain of human action. Aristotle, however, denies explicitly that Socrates dealt with nature as a whole. According to Aristotle, Socrates' interests were exclusively restricted to ethics.[250]

Furthermore, the passage in which the universality of (P18) is highlighted, (S51), contains expressions and ideas that are markedly Pythagorean. The reference to "the wise men," to the ideal of life in "community" which implies having things in common and being bound together by "friendship," the innovative step of calling the universe "cosmos," the interest in geometry and astronomy, and the attempt to conceive of a total system which includes all there is ("heaven and earth, gods and men") are some of the elements that strongly suggest ideas associated with the name of Pythagoras.[251]

But we are struck by the realization that there is hardly any evidence to connect the historical Socrates with the life and

thought of the Pythagorean sect.[252] Scholars of an earlier genera-
tion thought that the presence of two men from Thebes, Cebes and
Simmias, at Socrates' execution, who associated there with the
Pythagorean Philolaus, was a strong indication of Pythagorean
connections.[253] But there are persuasive reasons to suspect that the
two Thebans cannot be classed as Pythagoreans in any real
sense.[254] Moreover, in the middle Platonic dialogues and in the
Meno, Socrates displays an impressive expertise in mathematics, a
discipline justifiably associated with Pythagoras. But the Socrates
of the early dialogues gives no evidence of familiarity with, or of
interest in, the mathematical sciences.[255] Even the term *kosmos* is
used in the early period without any indication of its central role in
expressing a conception of the universe.[256]

Socrates never left Athens (except on military duty and for a
single trip to the isthmus of Corinth).[257] On the other hand, we
know that Plato traveled to Sicily on three occasions (the first time
probably before writing the *Gorgias* and the *Meno*), and that travel
to Sicily at that time meant passing through southern Italy along
the way. It is significant that the source for a view of the soul as
something radically different from the body—indeed as something imprisoned in the body, a view quite foreign to the early
dialogues but consistent with Pythagoreanism—is said to be "one
of the wise men" who in turn gives an allegorical interpretation of
a myth told by an "ingenious man" from Sicily or Italy.[258] We know
that Pythagorean communities flourished there, and we hear that
Plato initiated a long friendship with the Pythagorean Archytas of
Tarentum, a distinguished mathematician and active politician in
his city.[259] These biographical details suggest, I think, that the development of philosophical views under the influence of
Pythagorean thought should be attributed to the mature Plato
(rather than the historical Socrates).

If the foregoing is correct (given the nature of our sources, we
cannot be absolutely sure, of course), then it is reasonable to hold
that (P18), the new first principle designed to make Socratic ethics
rest upon a metaphysical foundation, was indeed introduced by
Plato.[260] And it is also reasonable to assert that Plato was the initiator of the natural law tradition in philosophy, if indeed we take its
defining characteristic to be the grounding of norms upon nature.[261]

Since Socrates did not attempt to make such a foundational

move, how would he have responded to the objection that the principles of his moral philosophy do not rest on a "natural" foundation, i.e., do not receive a justification based on objective principles governing reality as a whole?

Just as the Pythagorean references in the *Gorgias* are prospective (they anticipate and explain, among other things, the interest in the order of the soul and the city in the *Republic*), likewise some elements of the *Gorgias* look backwards and lead to a firmer grasp of the specifically Socratic system of ethics this book has been trying to discover in some of the early dialogues. We shall briefly examine this aspect of the *Gorgias* in the concluding section.

Conclusion

I hope these pages have managed to persuade the reader of a few things. One is that Socratic ethics advocates neither renunciation of one's personal happiness nor unqualified altruism. On the contrary, one of its defining features is its eudemonism, i.e., the view that individuals pursue their own happiness and, moreover, that it is good that they do so. Since it is rational to pursue one's own good, it would be irrational to give up one's own happiness. But this thesis does not transform it into a form of egoism in the usual sense of this term, i.e., in the sense that one ought to pursue one's own good even to the detriment of the good of others.

Why isn't Socratic eudemonism strictly egoistical? Because its second defining feature is its paradoxical way of determining what counts as one's own good, one's personal happiness. The ultimate good for an individual is the exercise of the moral excellences. But such exercise never leads to the detriment of the good of other people. When someone acts with the self-control, moderation, and reasonableness that correspond to the exercise of *sophrosyne*, that person attains a crucial personal good, but does not thereby deprive others of their good. As we saw in the previous chapter, *sophrosyne* entails justice, i.e., giving others their due. If I unduly keep a deposit and do not return it to my neighbor, I deprive him of his property, and by the same token I deprive myself of a good. The same holds, *mutatis mutandis*, for the exercise of piety: giving gods and parents their due does not make me worse off. Nor is courage (understood according to Socrates, not Callicles) an excellence that puts me at odds with others. On the contrary, remaining steadfast in the presence of danger and not fleeing, even at the risk of losing an important nonmoral good, namely life, is required for the protection of one's family, one's friends, and one's city.

We see that the Socratic pursuit of happiness in conjunction with the Socratic interpretation of happiness does not entail egoism. One's own flourishing requires active respect for the flourishing of others.

How did Socrates expect to persuade his fellow citizens that all of this is true? The historical arguments presented at the end of the previous chapter indicate that in all likelihood he did not invoke a deductive argument starting from a metaphysical premise and mediated by the notion of *kosmos* or the internal order of every being. The key is to be found in the sort of philosophical activity in which Socrates engaged in Athens and which we have already designated by its Greek name, the *elenchus*.

In the *Gorgias*, by means of the *elenchus* Socrates refutes Gorgias, Polus, and Callicles before he develops a positive, Platonic line of argument.

The operation of refuting his interlocutors consists in showing each of them that what they hold involves a contradiction. A close examination of their views leads to the discovery of two propositions that relate to each other as *p* does to *not p*.

If we leave aside the refutation of Gorgias, we have, in the case of Polus, the initial statement that it is better to do wrong than to suffer wrong, a statement contradicted by the conclusion that it is better to suffer wrong than to do wrong. At the outset Callicles holds that all pleasure is good; he is later forced to grant that some pleasures are good while some are not, i.e., that not all pleasure is good.

In order to achieve such results, Socrates asks each of his interlocutors to grant an intermediate proposition that leads to the contradictory of the initial proposition. In the conversation with Polus, that proposition claims that it is more shameful to do wrong than to suffer wrong. In the exchange with Callicles there is one "intermediate proposition" for each of the three arguments. I will focus here only on the first argument, where the damaging intermediate proposition is not explicitly formulated. Our analysis, though, shows that the intermediate proposition here must be that the pleasures of male prostitution or undue sexual submission are not good.

It has often been remarked that, from a strictly logical point of view, the initial proposition has not been proven false, nor the conclusion true, but only that they are inconsistent with each other. In each case, Polus or Callicles could have retracted the intermediate proposition and reaffirmed his initial convictions. Indeed, Callicles attempts to do this after the first antihedonistic argument, invoking the need for consistency with his original thesis.[262] But Socrates is quick to remark that this would imply lack of sincerity: deep in his soul, Callicles does not believe that the life of the *kinaidoi* is good.

In fact, Socrates presses the point that Polus and Callicles cannot sincerely abandon what I have called "the intermediate proposition." Four sections of the text strongly suggest this:[263]

(S52) Soc.: For I do believe that I, you [Polus], and everybody else thinks that to do wrong is worse than to suffer wrong, and that not to be punished [is worse] than to be punished.[264]

(S53) Soc.: Hence, what I was saying is true: that neither I, nor you [Polus], nor anybody else would rather do wrong than suffer wrong, for it happens to be worse.[265]

(S54) Soc.: . . . but if you leave this [= the thesis that to do wrong and escape punishment is the worst evil] unrefuted, by the dog, the god of the Egyptians! Callicles will not agree with you, Callicles, but will be discordant with you throughout your life. But I think, my excellent friend, that it is better for my lyre or the chorus I might lead, to be out of tune and discordant, or that the majority of men might disagree with me and contradict me, rather than, being only one individual, I should be discordant with myself and contradict myself.[266]

(S55) These [conclusions] [= that wrongdoing is worse and more shameful for the one who does wrong than for the one who suffers wrong] appeared to us earlier, [viz.] in the previous discussions [λόγοι], to be as I hold them to be. They are held firm and bound— even if it is a bit rude to say so—by arguments [λόγοι] of iron and adamant. At least so it seems. But if you or someone more vigorous than you does not untie them, no one who says something different from what I now hold can be speaking well [καλῶς λέγειν]. For I always say the same thing: that I do not know how these things are, but I have never run into someone capable of saying something different without making a fool of himself, as in the present case.[267]

Together, these passages suggest the following: Socrates values highly the logical consistency of the set of moral propositions an individual believes to be true. It is undesirable to have contradictory moral beliefs. Socrates also holds that while he does not have unshakable warranty of the truth of his own moral convictions, he has discovered through experience that it is always possible to show that anyone who denies one of these convictions thereby entertains contradictory beliefs and, as a result, makes a fool of himself. This explains why, *before refuting them*, Socrates can say to Polus that he, Polus, holds that it is worse to do wrong, and to Callicles that he is discordant with himself.

Why does Socrates expect from the outset that the *elenchus* will uncover a set of inconsistent beliefs in his interlocutors? Why not a set, perhaps a limited set, of false yet consistent beliefs? The most plausible reply I can suggest is that Socrates has a deep-rooted confidence in the power of human reason which manifests itself primarily in the grasp of the import of goodness. That is why human beings pursue what they see as good for themselves.[268] But human reason is not infallible in its discovery of what is good. We make mistakes. And yet, the power of human reason is such that mistakes do not always and inevitably occur. Even human beings whose practical rationality is seriously impaired or perverted do retain some correct evaluative beliefs. Thus, for example, while Callicles holds that self-control or chastity (*sophrosyne*) is bad for a man, he spontaneously admits that the lack of *sophrosyne* evinced in homosexual prostitution is bad.

The reason Callicles may have to believe that the practice of prostitution is detrimental to the agent, viz. that it may result in exclusion from the Assembly, is different from the reason Socrates would invoke, but the belief itself is consistent with Socratic ethics. This by itself does not guarantee that it is true. And yet, the fact that this particular belief contradicts Callicles' general rejection of *sophrosyne* shows that Callicles, insofar as he rejects one Socratic belief and accepts another one, holds contradictory beliefs. He cannot be "speaking well." His overall position is untenable. Socrates can be confident from the outset that this will be the case, because he is convinced that even Callicles will hold at least one true belief.

If it is possible to find within the set of beliefs of someone as radical as Callicles a view which Socrates deems correct, it should be easier for him to uncover acceptable views in the case of a weaker character (such as Polus) and, even more so, in the case of a political community. Life within the same *polis* is not possible if all the shared opinions about what is good and right are incorrect. The intermediate proposition granted by Polus belongs in this context. That to do something unjust is more shameful than to suffer injustice is a principle that a community must hold, at least for internal use, once it realizes that communal life is virtually impossible if the opposite principle is deemed true. A community that endorses and praises mutual aggression among its members cannot survive.

Would it be possible to design a system of ethics opposed to that of Socrates but endowed with internal consistency? The exploration of this abstract possibility seems to be foreign to his mission. He feels called to confront the actual thoughts of the individuals he meets and with whom he can debate. And many of those individuals, Socrates endeavors to show, do hold, as a matter of fact, inconsistent beliefs.

In sum, Socrates' ethics rests upon two and only two foundations. He did not attempt to justify them deductively, but he claimed that they yield—when supplemented by the definitions of the moral excellences—a complete and logically consistent system of moral philosophy. Those principles, as we saw, are:

> (P1) A choice is rational if and only if it is a choice of what is best for the agent,

and

> (P13) Something is good for an agent if and only if it is morally right.

From our discussion in chapter IV we know that (P13) does not exclude nonmoral goods, but it radically subordinates them to the moral virtues. Morally correct acquisition, possession, or use of a conditional good is not only a necessary condition for it to be a good; it is a sufficient condition as well. Wealth in the hands of a morally upright person can never harm her, nor can it benefit her in the absence of virtue. The contribution of the nonmoral goods to happiness is negligible.

We should finally note that the Socratic principles, if they are indeed true, have the advantage of providing us with something contemporary philosophers are deeply concerned about: reasons to be moral. If the good and the right coincide, then it is always in one's self-interest to do the morally right thing. Socrates showed his sincere commitment to this conclusion when he decided to stay in his cell and drink the hemlock. He had the strongest possible reason a rational agent can have to face death rather than disobey a court order. He did it for his own good and that of his fellow citizens.

Should we accept the Socratic principles from which such a paradoxical conclusion follows? Perhaps the best homage to Socratic irony would be to try to show that Socrates was wrong and that it is possible to derive a contradiction from his principles. Socrates himself invites us to do so:

> (S56) I will go through the argument [λόγος], then, the way it seems to me [right]. If it seems to any of you that I agree with myself on something which is not the case, you should interrupt and refute me [ἐλέγχειν], for I do not hold what I hold as someone who [already] knows. I am searching together with you, so that if the person who raises an objection seems to have a point, I shall be the first to concede it.[269]

APPENDIX

Socrates and Hedonism in the *Protagoras*

In the *Protagoras*, an early dialogue not directly considered in this book, Socrates makes certain statements that seem to commit him to the hedonistic position ["For I say that things are good insofar as they are pleasant if they have no consequences of another sort; and insofar as they are painful they are bad" (351c, Ostwald trans.)]. What is particularly striking is that the sophist initially rejects the hedonistic thesis and only reluctantly accepts it under pressure from Socrates (353e). The hedonistic thesis is then used as a premise to derive the Socratic denial of incontinence or *akrasia*, i.e., the impossibility for an agent to knowingly pursue what is bad. The generally accepted argument in favor of *akrasia* is that an agent can be seduced and overpowered by pleasure and thus do what he knows is bad (353a), but if pleasure is identical to the good, then absurd results follow.[1]

There has been disagreement among scholars on whether Socrates' statement of hedonism here expresses his sincere belief or is put forward strictly as a premise for an *ad hominem* argument.

In support of taking his statement at face value is the fact that the text does not seem to include words or terms which explicitly suggest that "the assumption is made for the sake of argument."[2] At one point, Vlastos also thought that "it is most unlikely that Socrates would deliberately offer a false proposition as a premise for establishing his great proposition, K [= "Knowledge is Virtue"]."[3] More recently, T. Irwin has tried to show that "hedonism is vital for Socrates' case [i.e., the rejection of incontinence]."[4]

Some time before his death, Vlastos arrived at a conception of Socratic irony which admits the possibility that Socrates made a misleading assertion, leaving it up to his interlocutor to find the truth by himself. Vlastos could then "firmly detach Socrates in the *Protagoras* from the hedonistic premise."[5] In my opinion, Zeyl has produced a persuasive analysis of the pertinent passages and arguments in the *Protagoras* which shows "the advantage the argument from hedonism has over the argument from [well-known Socratic doctrines] against a hedonistic opponent. And, [. . .] against such an opponent only."[6] If Zeyl is right, Socrates need not have espoused the hedonistic thesis himself. He certainly could have afforded to reject it.[7]

Indeed, in the absence of any evidence outside of the *Protagoras* for the hedonistic Socrates, and in the presence of vigorous antihedonistic argumentation in the *Gorgias* (and also in *Republic* VI 505b–c and *Philebus* 13a–c, 20c–21d), we would have to suppose not just one but two drastic changes of mind on the part of Plato in his portrayal of Socrates: first from the nonhedonistic philosopher of the *Apology* and *Crito* to the prohedonistic philosopher of the *Protagoras*, and from there to the antihedonistic thinker of the *Gorgias*. If the *Gorgias* antedates the *Protagoras* (as Kahn has argued),[8] the portrait would be even less persuasive, because then Socrates' hedonistic stage would follow a period of well-argued rejection of hedonism.

It is true that the earlier dialogues have neither endorsed nor rejected hedonism[9] in any explicit way, but (P3) ("an agent ought to consider *exclusively* whether his act will be just or unjust"), the principle that Socrates invokes both in the *Apology* and in the *Crito* to justify his most important decisions, is surely incompatible with a hedonistic strategy. If Socrates had calculated which of his options—to escape or to stay—would likely lead to more pleasure, we would have a radically different moral philosopher from the one presented in this book.

Notes

Introduction

1. A description of the sources for our knowledge of Socrates is provided by Guthrie (1971b). Since these sources contradict each other at different points, it is common to refer to the problem of the historical Socrates as "the Socratic question." In our century this question has gone through a period of deep skepticism, reflected in the books by Dupréel (1922), Gigon (1947), and Chroust (1957). On the other hand, Magalhães-Vilhena (1952) and others have argued in favor of Plato as a reliable source. On Gigon and Magalhães-Vilhena, cf. de Vogel (1951 and 1955). The Socratic question is summarized in the balanced article by A. R. Lacey (1971).

2. Most scholars divide Plato's dialogues into three periods (early, middle, and late) and usually hold that the early ones reflects Plato's recreation of the philosophy of Socrates. Cf. Vlastos (1991), pp. 46–47, and Benson (1992), pp. 4–6. Some of the key assumptions of the common view have been challenged by Kahn (1981) and are variously disputed at present. An account of the progress made in the chronological ordering of the dialogues starting in the second half of the nineteenth century appears in the introduction to Lledó et al. (1981), pp. 45–55. We find there, printed side by side, the roughly coincidental results obtained by eight scholars (Wilamowitz, Cornford, Leisegang, Praechter, Shorey, Ritter, Taylor, and Crombie). The use of computers has given a renewed impetus to chronological studies based on stylometric considerations. Brandwood (1976, pp. xiii–xvii, and 1990, pp. 249–252) claims to have established a firm sequence for the late dialogues (III) (*Timaeus, Critias, Sophist, Politicus, Philebus,* and *Laws*) and a highly reliable one for the dialogues he places in the middle group (II) (*Republic, Parmenides, Theaetetus,* and *Phaedrus*). In relative proximity to the middle dialogues stand the following dialogues from Brandwood's group (IB): *Phaedo, Lysis, Symposium, Cratylus, Menexenus, Euthydemus,* and *Hippias Major.* This group also includes the

Gorgias and the *Meno*, which is the latest of the early dialogues, in virtually everyone's opinion. Apart from this, little can be said on the basis of stylometry about the sequence of dialogues within the early group. Brandwood's earliest group (IA) includes (in alphabetical order): *Apology*, *Charmides*, *Crito*, *Euthyphro*, *Hippias Minor*, *Ion*, *Laches*, and *Protagoras*. In the present book the chief chronological assumptions are that the *Apology* and the *Crito* are quite early and that the *Gorgias* was written after Plato's first trip to Italy and Sicily [cf. Dodds (1959), pp. 25–27]. This allows for an interlude of eight to thirteen years to accommodate the important shift in the justification of Socratic ethics defended in chapter V, *infra*.

3.   The Aristotelian passages on Socrates have been collected by Deman (1942).

4.   For an overview cf. White (1968).

5.   E.g., *Memorabilia* 3. 9. 4–5 (cf. 4. 2. 19–23), and *Gorgias* 460a ff. For a persuasive explanation of this paradoxical doctrine cf. Santas (1982), pp. 183–194.

6.   *Nicomachean Ethics* 9. 8. 1169a 17: πᾶς γὰρ νοῦς αἱρεῖται τὸ βέλτιστον ἑαυτῷ.

7.   E.g. Glassen (1957).

8.   Adkins (1960) has provided a provocative account of that development. He has been criticized by Lloyd-Jones (1983) and Long (1970). An excellent study of the basic problems involved is Creed (1973).

9.   In Vlastos (1984), p. 181, p. 202 n. 3; and Vlastos (1991), p. 200, it is argued that Socrates assumed this canon of five and only five moral virtues. Socrates also held that, strictly speaking, these virtues constitute a unity. For a clear and concise formulation of the doctrine and its possible interpretations, cf. Penner (1973). See also Woodruff (1976) and Ferejohn (1982).

10.   The best-known defender of (1) is T. Irwin. His views have been opposed by G. Vlastos, who has shifted from (2a) to (2b). There was a memorable exchange between these two scholars in 1978 in the *Times Literary Supplement* (Feb. 24, March 17, April 21, May 5, June 9, June 16, July 14, Aug. 4, and Sept. 3). Cf. also Irwin (1977), Vlastos (1984), and Zeyl (1982).

Chapter I

11.   On the structure of the Socratic *elenchus*, cf. Vlastos (1983a) with comments by Kraut (1983). See also Stemmer (1992), esp. pp. 96–127.

12.   *Republic* I, 337a 3–7. At *Apology* 23a 3–5 Socrates admits that people consistently perceived him as "wise" in those subjects in which they saw

him refuting someone. For all quotations from Plato I have used Burnet (1900–1907) as my main source. Translations are my own unless otherwise noted. In the renderings I have aimed almost exclusively at accuracy, even at the price of neglecting the elegance and flexibility of Plato's style. Readers are encouraged to consult the main sources in excellent translations by Grube (1981) and Zeyl (1987).

13.   Vlastos (1991), pp. 21–30, conjectures that the modern sense of the term "irony," which in Western rhetorical theory goes back to Cicero and Quintilian, is ultimately due to Socrates. Before him the meaning of *eroniea* and its cognates almost always implied an intention to deceive.

14.   *Symp.* 218d 6–219a 1. Cf. Vlastos (1991), p. 36.

15.   *Symp.* 219a 1–2.

16.   *Symp.* 216e 6–217a 1.

17.   *Apol.* 24b 8–c 1. I have added bracketed letters to make references more expedient. The evidence for this being virtually the official wording of the indictment is a statement in *Diogenes Laertius* (2. 40) which claims that Favorinus, a Roman rhetorician of the second century A.D., reported that it was still preserved in the sanctuary of the Mother of the Gods in Athens. On the meaning of the accusations, see Brickhouse and Smith (1989), pp. 30–37, and Reeve (1989), pp. 74–79.

18.   *Apol.* 19b 4–c 1.

19.   *Apol.* 18b 7. Cf. Burnet (1924), *ad loc.*

20.   Cf. Cornford (1952), pp. 127–142.

21.   Thuc. 8. 65. 2. Cf. *Meno* 89e–95a. For a lively account of the general historical background (and of Alcibiades in particular), cf. Burn (1966), pp. 193–304.

22.   On the assumed influence of Gorgias of Leontini on Alcibiades, cf. Guthrie (1971b), p. 274.

23.   The label "corruptor of youth" has moral connotations both in Greek and in English. It singles out the person who leads the young from moral virtue to vice. Xenophon stresses this aspect of the accusations: Xen. *Apol.* 19 and *Mem.* 1. 2. 1–5. Cf. *Mem.* 1. 5. 1–6.

24.   *Apol.* 19d.

25.   *Apol.* 19c 4–8.

26.   *Apol.* 19d 8–20c 3.

27.   *Apol.* 20c 4–d 4.

28.   *Apol.* 21a 4–7.

29.   *Apol.* 21b 4–5.

30.   *Apol.* 21b 6–7. The claim that the god is subject to a superior moral order represented by *themis*, the divine order of the universe, is quite strong. Cf. Hirzel (1907) and Ehrenberg (1921).

31. Cf. Heraclitus Frg. B93 (Diels-Kranz): "The Lord to whom the oracle that is in Delphi belongs neither speaks out plainly nor conceals, but gives hints." On some of the famous ambiguous replies given by the oracle, cf. Fontenrose (1978).

32. *Apol.* 21b 3–4: "What is the god saying? What is his riddle?" Cf. 21e 6.

33. *Apol.* 21c d.

34. *Pace* Lesher (1987), p. 281. Cf. 22d 2 where the craftsmen are said to know many fine things (*kala*). The implication is surely that they possess not moral knowledge but the kind of knowledge required for the successful exercise of their crafts.

35. *Apol.* 22a 8–c 3.

36. *Apol.* 22c 5–6.

37. On specific claims to knowledge extrapolated from poetic inspiration, cf. Plato's *Ion* and Flashar (1958).

38. *Apol.* 22d 3–e 1.

39. On this point I side with Burnet (1924), p. 96, and against Brickhouse and Smith (1989), p. 97, and Reeve (1989), p. 33. I find it hard to believe that Socrates is here implying that, e.g., good carpenters walk around the *agora* claiming to know the definition of a handful of moral virtues. The expression "the greatest things" should be understood here from the perspective of those who allegedly make the claim. The average Athenian citizen surely felt that political issues were the most important ones and that he was competent to deal with them.

40. For the close linkage of the two, cf. *Apol.* 23d 5–24a 1.

41. Cf. *Phaedo* 96a–102a. The correct historical interpretation of this "autobiography" is still one of the most vexing problems for Platonic scholars who raise the Socratic question.

42. *Apol.* 26d 6–e 1. Socrates appears to be familiar with some doctrines of Anaxagoras, a philosopher from Asia Minor who was a friend of Pericles, but in the same passage he makes it known that such information was readily available to anyone, for Anaxagoras' book could be purchased for a modest price at the *agora*.

43. Burnet (1924), pp. 50–51, argues against taking *Euthyphro* 11b as proof that Socrates (and/or his father) was a stonemason. The earliest reference to Socrates as a stonecutter goes back to Timon of Phlius, a skeptic philosopher who lived in the third century B.C.

44. Cf. *Gorgias* 521d 6–8. Cf. Dodds's comment *ad loc.*: "One may doubt, however, whether the historical Socrates would have made any such claim."

45. Cf. *Rep.* 473 c–d; 484b.

124   *Notes*

46. "Politics" should be understood in this sense at *Gorgias* 473e 6 where Socrates *denies* being a politician. This claim and the opposite one made at 521d (quoted above) do not contradict each other.

47. Cf. *Apol.* 20b 4–5. Cf. *Protagoras* 318e 5–319a 5; *Meno* 73c 6–9.

48. *Apol.* 29a 6–b 6.

49. At the end of the *Apology* (40c ff.), Socrates conjectures that there is hope (*elpis*) that death is something good, for it is either like a dreamless night or, if (religious) tales are true, like a migration to a better place. Expressing such hope is not tantamount to claiming knowledge.

50. *Apol.* 24a 6–8.

51. *Apol.* 37d 6–7.

52. *Apol.* 21b 4–5.

53. *Apol.* 22b 9–d 1. I owe this reference and the four preceding ones to Lesher (1987), p. 280.

54. *Apol.* 29b 6–9.

55. When the claim that wrongdoing is bad and shameful is repeated in the *Crito* (49b 4), the qualification "for the wrongdoer" is introduced immediately before the term "bad." This seems to count in favor of the interpretation defended above. Moral predicates are true or false without qualification. Nonmoral benefit usually requires specification: what is good for me may be bad for you (e.g., my getting a job for which both of us have applied). To hold that doing wrong is bad *for the one who does it*, is, of course, paradoxical.

56. I am assuming that, with normal Greek usage, καλόν ("fine," "admirable," "noble," "beautiful") is the opposite of αἰσχρόν and can be used to convey moral commendation.

57. *Rep.* I. 354c 1–3. Some nineteenth-century scholars argued on the basis of stylistic evidence that Book I of the *Republic* was an independent dialogue written during Plato's earlier years that was later used as the opening section of a more mature work that includes Books II–X. Vlastos has argued that independently of the truth or falsehood of this thesis, the Socrates of Book I in fact shares most of his traits with the Socrates of the early dialogues. Cf. Vlastos (1991), chapter 2, *passim*, and pp. 248–251. The separate composition of Book I has been vigorously contested by Kahn (1993).

58. Cf. *Euthydemus* 279a 1–3; 280b 5–6; *Symp.* 204e 1–7.

59. *Laches* 192c 5–7; *Charmides* 159c 1–2.

60. At *Gorgias* 492a–c, Callicles, a strong opponent of Socrates, makes an effort to explain why in everyday life "the many" (*hoi polloi*, 492a 3) praise justice. This habit is due, in his opinion, to sheer cowardice. But the need of an explanation simply confirms the view that categorizing justice as a virtue was commonplace for fifth- and fourth-century Greeks.

61. Cf. *Euth.* 4a 11–12.

62. *Euth.* 4e 4–5a 2.

63. Cf. Aristotle, *Nicomachean Ethics* 1. 2. 1104a 1–2.

64. *Euth.* 5d 8–e 2.

65. *Euth.* 5d 1–5; 6d 9–e 1.

66. *Euth.* 6e 3–6.

67. *Euth.* 5a 3–b 7; 5c 4–5; 15e 5–16a 4.

68. *Euth.* 11e 4–12e 8.

69. *Euth.* 12e 5–8; 13d 4.

70. *Apol.* 30a 5–7 (trans. Vlastos). Cf. Vlastos (1991), p. 175.

71. *Crito* 48b 3–10.

72. Cf. *Crito* 46b 6–c 6.

73. This silence probably reflects a lack of interest in strictly epistemological questions on the part of the historical Socrates. The first attempts to deal with this problem are found in *Gorgias* 454c ff. and in the transition dialogues. Cf. *Meno* 98a.

74. *Apol.* 20d 6–e 3.

75. *Apol.* 23a 5–b 4.

Chapter II

76. Cf. Barker (1977), p. 27: "While it may be that a given law has no specifically moral content, the system of law in general, which constitutes the framework of the πόλις, is a moral system, and breaches in it are thus *ipso facto* moral breaches: they are ἄδικα, ἀνόσια." In the attempt to identify the moral ideas implicit in the *Apology*, I owe much to Santas (1982), pp. 20–43.

77. Cf. Santas (1982), p. 32. Allen (1980), p. 29, seems to hold that Socrates did not deny the charges leveled against him. This claim appears to be untenable in the light of *Apol.* 24c–28a, a lengthy portion of the speech in which both corruption of youth and impiety are rejected. It ends with a statement summarizing what Socrates takes to have accomplished: "In fact, Athenians, that I am not guilty in conformity with the deposition of Meletus does not seem to me to require a lengthy defense: what I have said is enough." One should also not miss the dramatic force of one of the final statements before the vote which could have left him a free man: "For I honor them [= the gods], Athenians, like none of my accusers."

78. *Apol.* 28b 3–9.

79. *Apol.* 28d 4–10. On the use of *aischron*, cf. (S16), above, and the corresponding comments.

80. *Apol.* 28d 10–29a 1.

81. *Apol.* 29b 9–c 1 and c 5–d 5.

82. *Euth.* 5e 5–6c 8. Our chief source for the deeds of Zeus and Cronus is Hesiod, *Theogony*, 453–465 and 176–182. On the *peplos* or robe of Athena, cf. *Rep.* 378b–c.

83. *Euth.* 7a–9e.

84. *Euth.* 10a 2–3.

85. *Euyh.* 10d 4–5.

86. *Euth.* 10e 9–11a 4. This somewhat convoluted yet persuasive argument has been ably analysed by Cohen (1971).

87. *Euth.* 11a 6–b 1.

88. Cf. *Euth.* 6e 3–6.

89. Thus a deontological system defines the right independently of the nonmoral good, whereas a teleological one defines the right by reference to an independently defined nonmoral good. These definitions have been adapted from Frankena (1963), pp. 14–15; and Rawls (1971), pp. 24 and 30. Cf. Cooper (1975), pp. 87–88. I have made no effort to make one kind of system the strict denial of the other one.

90. *Apol.* 30c 6–d 5.

91. Not only will the accusers be harmed but the rest of the Athenians as well, for they will be deprived of the good of having Socrates as a gadfly to stir them toward the care for virtue, which is, on the above assumptions, in their best interest. Cf. *Apol.* 30e–31a.

Chapter III

92. Xenophon, *Apol.* 23.

93. Cf. Xenophon, *Mem.* IV. 8. 2.

94. *Phaedo* 58a 6–c 5. Since a fortunate coincidence or *tyche* can be readily interpreted by a Greek as the deed of a god, the use of the cognate verbal form τύχωσιν in the text suggests in a veiled manner that Apollo gave Socrates a reprieve first by letting the mission begin before the trial and then by preventing the ship from returning swiftly to Athens.

95. *Crito* 45a–c.

96. Cf. *Crito* 44b–46a.

97. *Crito* 46a 3–4.

98. Cf. *Crito* 45e 2, 6. *Ananadria* is, literally, "unmanliness."

99. *Crito* 46b 3–c 6.

100. *Symp.* 220c 3–d 5. Cf. also *Symp.* 174d–175c, where we find a similar, quasi-ecstatic experience which befalls Socrates when he is on his way to the house of the poet Agathon. It is said there that "he has this particular

habit or custom" (ἔθος γάρ τι τοῦτ' ἔχει, 175b 1–2). We should bear in mind, however, that the ecstatic Socrates, the eloquent speaker who narrates grandiose myths and transmits a sublimated interpretation of the erotic ascension to the Forms, is the Socrates of the middle dialogues. He is remarkably different from the Socrates of the early ones.

101. Cf. Xenophon, *Apol.* 4–5, 12–13; *Symp.* 8. 5; *Mem.* 1. 1. 2–4; 4. 8. 1 and 5. For indirect allusions cf. also *Apol.* 8 and *Mem.* 4. 3. 12.

102. Cf. Guthrie (1971b), pp. 82–85, and Gundert (1954), *passim.*

103. *Apol.* 31c 7–d 5.

104. *Apol.* 40a 3–c 3. Burnet *ad loc.* translates the last words quoted (*ti agathon praxein*) by "to fare well in some way."

105. Cf. *Apol.* 32a–b (with Burnet's notes *ad loc.*); Xenophon, *Hellenica* 1. 7. 4–35. Cf. further Wilamowitz-Moellendorff (1919), vol. I, p. 101.

106. *Apol.* 31d 6–32a 2.

107. This conviction becomes stronger toward the end of the proceedings. Cf. *Apol.* 41d 3 6: "But this is clear to me that to die now and be released from my troubles is better for me. That is why the sign didn't oppose me at any point."

108. The divine sign is also mentioned in *Euth.* 3b 5–7; *Euthydemus* 272e 3–4; *Rep.* 6. 496c 3–4; *Phaedrus* 242b 8–9 and *Theaet.* 151a 4. Cf. Brickhouse and Smith (1989), p. 35, n. 126.

109. Xenophon, *Apol.* 12.

110. *Mem.* 4. 8. 1. Cf. further 1. 1. 4. In the first of these passages Xenophon provides an answer to the charge that the sign deceived Socrates because he was in fact condemned to death. Xenophon argues that it was in Socrates' best interest to die because through death he would escape the pains and senility that accompany old age.

111. *Mem.* 1. 1. 9 (Marchant trans. slightly modified).

112. *Crito* 47a–c.

113. *Crito* 47c 9–10.

114. *Crito* 47e 7.

115. *Crito* 47c–48a.

116. *Crito* 48b 11–d 5. The expression translated as "to take into account *x* instead of *y*" (ὑπολογίζεσθαι . . . πρό) can be paraphrased as "to give countervailing weight to *x* when the alternative is *y*." Cf. Vlastos (1984), pp. 186–187. The same expression appeared twice in (S22).

117. *Crito* 49b 8. The modal expression "in no way" (οὐδαμῶς) may be taken as roughly equivalent to "never." The particle *ara* in the Greek shows that this is a conclusion from statements that appear earlier in the text, presumably starting at 48a 5. Hence, although it may be taken as a principle for action, it is not a principle in an unqualified sense, i.e., an

underived proposition.

118. *Crito* 49b 4–6 and *Apol.* 29b 6–7. The modal expression "in every way" here may again be understood as equivalent to a temporal adverb such as "always."

119. *Crito* 49b 10 ff.

120. *Crito* 49c 7–8. Cf. Barker (1977), p. 16.

121. *Crito* 49e 9–50a 3.

122. In light of the gender of the Latin noun *lex* from which the English term "law" is derived, we are naturally inclined to imagine the personified laws as women. In Greek, however, "law" is masculine (ὁ νόμος). Hence, the appropriate visual image is that of Crito and Socrates surrounded by a group of men (perhaps not too different from the bearded elders on the north section of the Parthenon frieze). Cf. Ashmole (1972), p. 135, fig. 154, and Andronicos (1981), p. 77, fig. 75. It should be noted that what is being personified are, more precisely, "the laws and the common(wealth) of the city" (τὸ κοινόν τῆς πόλεως). This expression indicates that we are dealing here not with peripheral norms but with the very core of the Athenian legal system.

123. *Crito* 50a 8–b 5.

124. *Crito* 50b 5–9. On the function of the orator mentioned here, cf. Burnet (1924), *ad loc.*

125. Woozley (1971) has interpreted the argument roughly along these lines and has been criticized by Barker (1977). My views on the subject owe much to Barker.

126. Cf. Crito 50b 4–5 where the Greek stresses these two ideas (μηδὲν ἰσχύωσιν, ἄκυροί γίγνωνται).

127. Crito 50b 5 (διαφθείρωνται), 7–8 (τούτου τοῦ νόμου ἀπολλυμένου).

128. Cf. *Crito* 50a 6–7.

129. The transition is effected in 50c–51c.

130. *Crito* 51c 6–52d 5.

131. *Crito* 51e 7.

132. *Crito* 54b 8–c 1.

133. *Crito* 51b 3–4; 51b 9–c 1 and 51e 4–52a 3.

134. The disjunction is exclusive in a nonstandard sense because the joint satisfaction of both disjuncts is empty. If you obey there is no need to persuade, and if you persuade there will be no unwelcome orders to be obeyed.

135. *Crito* 51b 8–9. Obedience in war and (vaguely) "everywhere else" is also mentioned.

136. *Crito* 51c 1.

137. Cf. *Crito* 51b 5–6.

138. For a different interpretation, see Kraut (1984), pp. 54–90.

139. Cf. *Apol.* 32c 3–d 7.

140. Cf. Kraut (1984), pp. 13–17.

141. Cf. *Apol.* 29b 6–7.

142. The alleged inconsistency between the *Apology* and the *Crito* has been rejected on the basis of detailed argumentation in Santas (1982), pp. 10–56.

143. *Crito* 48b 3–c 1.

144. Cf. note 89 *supra*. Cooper (1975), pp. 87–88, has made a similar claim for Aristotelian ethics. Under the current definition of teleological ethics, Aristotle's position is not strictly teleological either, because his concept of happiness includes the moral goods. But it also includes nonmoral goods, e.g., the excellent exercise of theoretical reason. In his ethics, therefore, the right and the good do not fully coincide. This marks an important difference between Socratic and Aristotelian ethics.

Chapter IV

145. Cf. *Gorgias* 481c 1–4. The arguments in the *Gorgias* have been analyzed by Santas (1982), pp. 218–303. The present interpretation owes much to Kahn (1983).

146. *Gorgias* 447a–461b. For general information on Gorgias, see Guthrie (1971a). The Greek text of Gorgias' extant works is printed in Diels-Kranz (1956) and a complete translation appears in Sprague (1972).

147. *Gorgias* 461b–481b.

148. *Gorgias* 481b–527e. Scholars have debated whether this character, remarkable for his vigor and the boldness of his moral conceptions, is (a) Plato's own invention, (b) a mask to disguise some well-known historical figure (such as Critias or Alcibiades), or (c) a historical individual about whom we do not know from other sources due to some mishap (he may have died early enough not to have made a name for himself in Athens). Cf. Guthrie (1971a), p. 102, n. 1. Since he belongs to a known deme (495d) and has a beloved (481d) and friends (487c) whose historicity is attested, I am inclined to accept the third alternative as correct. See also Irwin (1979), p. 110, and Kerferd (1981), p. 119. Furthermore, in the dialogues there do not seem to be characters with a proper name (as opposed, e.g., to "the guest from Elea" or "the Athenian") who are not historical figures. The priestess Diotima from the remote town of Mantinea mentioned in the *Symposium* appears to be an exception, but she does not speak there *in propria persona*. It could also well be that someone by that name did exist.

What is highly unlikely is that she would have had an accurate understanding of a sophisticated metaphysical theory developed about four or five decades after she allegedly instructed Socrates on matters of love.

149.   *Gorgias* 523a–527e. This is surely a novelty in the chronological order of the dialogues, and in the text Socrates presents the myth as something heard from an unnamed informant (524a 8). "This is certainly," according to Dodds (1959), p. 373, "in part at least, a device to avoid making Socrates responsible for opinions which he did not in fact hold." In chapter V we shall see further indications of Plato's distancing himself from his predecessor.

150.   *Gorgias* 456c–457c. In contrast with Protagoras of Abdera and other sophists, Gorgias did not officially advertise himself as a teacher of *arete*, i.e., of the quality that would make the student a good individual and thus unlikely to misuse a neutral skill. Cf. *Meno* 95c and Guthrie (1971a), p. 271.

151.   *Gorgias* 459c 8–e 9.

152.   *Gorgias* 460a 3–4.

153.   *Gorgias* 460a–c. This argument from the crafts to the sufficiency of knowledge for moral excellence is one of the most striking statements of so-called Socratic intellectualism. At first sight the argument seems to be fallacious (i.e., to involve true premises and a false conclusion), because we think moral virtue is analogous to the crafts in some respects but not in others. The chief disanalogy is, of course, that the practice of virtue seems to require something beyond mere knowledge. To be a carpenter one has to know what carpenters know; to be virtuous one has to know what is right and also have a firm disposition to act on it. We admit that people do things they know to be bad and fail to do things that they know to be good or even obligatory. But Socrates' argument seems to assume supplementary premises which do make it valid. Cf. below, p. 81–82, and Irwin (1982), p. 127.

154.   *Gorgias* 461b–c.

155.   By 462d it is really Socrates who is once again leading the conversation: he suggests to Polus what he should ask.

156.   *Gorgias* 465a. The passage is obscure because of a corruption of the Greek text. I follow Dodds (1959), pp. 229–230.

157.   Cf. Dodds (1959), p. 226. The interest in abstract and complete classifications, the prominence of mathemtical proportion between the different items, and, last but not least, the attribution to Socrates of a lengthy speech are symptomatic of the distance Plato gradually places between himself and the historical Socrates.

158.   *Gorgias* 466a–b.

159.   In several Greek cities of Sicily, tyranny had been the predominant political regime since the beginning of the fifth century. It is often argued

that, given the permanent threat of a Carthaginian invasion, this was the only viable solution for the preservation of the Sicilian Greeks. Cf. Bury-Meiggs (1975), pp.186–193 and 385–413.

160. Cf. *Gorgias* 448c, 462b 3–c 1, and Aristotle, *Met.* 1. 1. 981 a 4 (who probably refers back to the *Gorgias*).

161. *Gorgias* 466b 6–7.

162. Representatives of Athens assert this in Thucydides 5. 95. 1.

163. *Gorgias* 466b 11–c 2. Cf. 466c 9–d 3. The Greek expression at the end of (S39) is an impersonal phrase which is commonly used to record the decisions of a public body. Many Athenian inscriptions begin with the words ἔδοξη τῇ βουλῇ καὶ τῷ δήμῳ, "it was resolved by the Council and the People." Thus, the last clause in (S39) could be rendered by "whoever they decide," "whoever they see fit." But the context suggests that Socrates takes the expression to be elliptical for "what seems to them to be best" (cf., e.g., 466e 1). With this supplement, the meaning of the verb shifts from an emphasis on decision to an emphasis on opinion or belief. Given that beliefs, but not decisions, can be true or false, it will become clear why the argument requires a rendering of the Greek that mentions "seeming," "believing," "thinking," or some such verb.

164. *Gorgias* 466e 1–2 and 467b 2.

165. *Gorgias* 467c 5–7.

166. *Gorgias* 467e 1–468a 3.

167. For a different interpretation cf. Irwin (1979), p. 141. In chapter 4 of Book III of the *Nicomachean Ethics* Aristotle discusses the difficulties involved in linking the will to the real good or the apparent good. There is no explicit mention of Socrates in the context, but the Aristotelian alternatives correspond closely to the passage analyzed above.

168. This rather unrealistic possibility is defended by Thrasymachus in Book I of the *Republic*. Cf. *Rep.* 340d–341a.

169. *Gorgias* 468e 6–9.

170. *Gorgias* 468e 10–469c 2.

171. *Gorgias* 470e 8–11.

172. *Meno* 77b–78b. Since (P16) makes its appearance at this stage in the chronological order of the dialogues and is later echoed at *Rep.* 505d–e, it is plausible to conjecture that it represents a more refined formulation on the part of Plato of a principle required to justify Socratic intellectualism.

173. *Gorgias* 460b 6–8.

174. Cf. McTighe (1984).

175. Cf. *Gorgias* 509e 5–7.

176. I owe my awareness of this problem to Vlastos (1984).

177. Since Socrates is here enumerating generally acknowledged goods

and is not arguing for his own list, I am inclined to take *sophia* in its ordinary sense of "expertise in a craft" or, more generally, "mental shrewdness," a talent useful in any domain. Cf. Aristotle, *Nicomachean Ethics* 6. 7. 1141a 9–14.

178. *Gorgias* 467e 4–5.

179. *Euthydemus* 279a 4–c 2. It is useful to compare this passage with Aristotelian enumerations of goods in *Rhetoric* 1. 5. 1360 b 18–30 and 1. 6. 1362 b 10–28.

180. Cf. *Laches* 195a, *Charmides* 165c, and *Meno* 89a 3–4.

181. Cf. Aristotle, *Nicomachean Ethics*, Book VI, chapter 5.

182. *Euthydemus* 281d 8 and 279c 2–280a 7.

183. *Euthydemus* 280b 5–6 (εὐδαιμονεῖν . . . καὶ εὖ πράττειν).

184. *Euthydemus* 280d 6.

185. *Euthydemus* 281b 4–8.

186. *Euthydemus* 281c 6–7.

187. Cf. *Meno* 88b 3–5: "Take the case of courage, if courage is not wisdom (*phronesis*), but a form of recklessness. When a man is reckless without knowledge (*nous*), isn't he harmed; but with knowledge, doesn't he benefit?" *Meno* 87e 5–89a 7 is a close parallel to the passage we are discussing.

188. *Euthydemus* 281d 3–4.

189. *Euthydemus* 281d 2–e 1.

190. Parmenides, one of the most influential philosophers before Socrates, holds that there exists only one entity, called Being (τὸ ἐόν), which "remains the same . . . by itself" (ταὐτόν . . . καθ' ἑαυτό) (B8. 29), i.e., in total solitude. In *Meno* 88c 6, a passage closely linked to our section of the *Euthydemus*, the adverbial phrase αὐτὰ . . . καθ' αὑτά, appears in a reference to things in the soul which in themselves are neither beneficial nor detrimental.

191. *Gorgias* 468a 1–3.

192. A slightly different reconstruction is put forward in Vlastos (1984), p. 201.

193. *Crito* 47d 7–e 5.

194. *Apol.* 30b 2–4 (Grube translation).

195. Burnet (1924) *ad loc.*, p. 124, had shown that the word order is misleading and that the predicate is *agatha tois anthropois*, "goods for men." The correct rendering appears in Cornford (1932), p. 36, and has also been defended by Vlastos (1984), p. 193.

196. *Gorgias* 469b 8 (S41).

197. *Gorgias* 470e 7–11 (S42).

198. It may be objected that morally correct use is a necessary but not a sufficient condition for something like wealth to be good, because beyond a certain point I may have no use for further wealth. But as long as it is right for me to have it or eventually to use it, wealth cannot be something bad for me. Conditional goods on Socrates' view are radically dependent on the unconditional ones.

199. *Gorgias* 473a 7 and 474c 5–6.

200. *Gorgias* 474c 7–8.

201. *Gorgias* 474c 9–d 2.

202. Cf. Liddell & Scott (1953), *s.v. kalos*, Santas (1982), p. 236, and Kahn (1983), p. 94.

203. *Gorgias* 475a 4–5. Note the subtle transition from "useful" to "beneficial" to "good" in the previous exchanges.

204. On this problem cf. Vlastos (1967), *passim*.

205. Cf. Kahn (1983), pp. 92–94.

206. *Gorgias* 474a 5–6. On this topic cf. Mackenzie (1981).

207. Cf. *Gorgias* 474 a 5–6: "For I [= Soc.] know how to present only one witness [in support of] whatever I am saying: the man with whom I am discussing."

Chapter V

208. Cf. Heinimann (1945); and Guthrie (1971a), chapter IV, pp. 55–134.

209. Cf. Aristotle's comments in *De Sophisticis Elenchis* 173a 7–18, especially lines 14–16, on the Calliclean superiority of the natural over the customary: "In their view [= that of Callicles and the older sophists] the standard of nature was the truth, while that of convention was the opinion held by the majority" (Revised Oxford Translation, Barnes [1984]).

210. As Heinimann (1945), pp. 123–124 suggests, the change from the singular to the plural of the word *nomos* reflects a conceptual step from received custom to statutory legislation. Cf. further Dodds (1959), p. 266.

211. The invasion of Greece by the Persian king Xerxes is the theme of Herodotus, Books VII–IX, while Darius' campaign in Scythia is chronicled by Herodotus in Book IV, 1–144. The irony of having Callicles give these two examples should not be missed: both campaigns ended in total failure.

212. *Gorgias* 482c 4–484b 1. In most textual matters I have followed Dodds (1959). I have borrowed a phrase or two from the translations of Irwin (1979) and Zeyl (1987). On the essentials of Callicles' position, cf. Kerferd (1981), pp. 117–120.

213. Cf. Dodds (1959), p. 266.

214. Cf. Irwin (1979), p. 178.

215. *Gorgias* 492b.

216. *Gorgias* 491e 8.

217. *Gorgias* 492c 5–6.

218. *Gorgias* 491e 8–492a 3.

219. *Gorgias* 491e 7.

220. *Gorgias* 492e 8–b 1.

221. *Gorgias* 492c 7.

222. On the origins of the natural law idea in poetry and pre-Socratic thought cf. Ehrenberg (1923). Finnis (1980) offers a contemporary version of the natural law approach.

223. *Pace* Kerferd (1981), p. 118, I think it is impossible to decide whether or not Callicles is committing "the naturalistic fallacy," i.e., whether Plato wants us to understand Callicles' position as an illegitimate move from what is the case to what ought to be the case. The text does suggest that the general rule of natural justice is somehow based on an induction from what goes on among animals and men.

224. It has often been observed that there is a striking similarity between the wording of Callicles' statement on natural justice and a claim made by Athenian representatives in Thucydides' Melian Dialogue (*History of the Peloponnesian War* 5. 105. 2). The Athenians argue that the weaker Melians should surrender because gods and men, driven by natural necessity (ὑπὸ φύσεως ἀναγκαίας, "by a necessary nature"), always rule over those who are weaker than themselves. The Athenian negotiators add, moreover, that this is a *nomos* they did not enact but that holds forever. Nevertheless, we should note an important difference between these two versions of "natural law." While Callicles makes the *moral* claim that it is just for the strong to dominate the weak, the Athenians make a purely factual claim. They hold that, as a matter of fact, the strong always dominate the weak. They refrain from making any moral or evaluative statement about this general rule. For a detailed study of this contrast see Gómez-Lobo (1991).

225. *Crito* 47a–48a.

226. *Gorgias* 488d 1–489b 6.

227. *Gorgias* 491b 1–4. The question whether strength may be an intellectual attribute and not a physical one was raised by Socrates at 489e 7–8. Callicles immediately jumped on the suggestion and endorsed it as his own.

228. *Gorgias* 491d 4–e 1.

229. *Gorgias* 492c 8.

230. On the claim that Socrates himself (or Plato) was a hedonist at a

certain stage of his philosophical development, see Appendix: Socrates and hedonism in the *Protagoras*.

231. I owe much here to Kahn (1983). The rigorous arguments against hedonism are preceded in the text by a myth that Socrates claims to have heard from "one of the wise men" who in turn got it from "some clever man, either a Sicilian or an Italian." Its central idea is that the human body is a tomb of the soul which is thus condemned to satisfy insatiable physical desires. Cf. Dodds (1959), pp. 296–299. Below I provide a context for this myth and its implications.

232. Rowe (1976), p. 49. Notice that Rowe adds: "the Greek word [*kinaidos*] seems to have a more specific meaning, but I am unable to discover what that meaning is."

233. Dover (1978).

234. Cf. Kahn (1983), pp. 106–107. This should not be taken to mean that every form of genital homosexual contact was considered illicit or unlawful. If Dover is right, some forms of homosexual coitus were acceptable, namely those that did not involve passive submission to the lover.

235. *Phaedo* 60b–c. Cf. Dodds (1959), p. 309. Plato returned to the problem of pleasure in the *Republic* (especially 580d–588a) and in the *Philebus*, *passim*. Cf. Grube (1935), pp. 51–86.

236. *Gorgias* 503e 1–504b 6. I translate the text as established by Dodds.

237. As we saw in chapter II, *taxis* is a word applied primarily to the order and disposition of an army. It often denotes a single line of soldiers and thus the drawing up of the men in rank and file. Our word "tactics" is derived from the corresponding verb. *Kosmos* is often used in the adverbial phrase *kata kosmon* to express the appropriate or due order of a thing or action. For the sake of economy in setting out the argument, I use "order" for both *taxis* and *kosmos*.

238. *Gorgias* 504c 7–d 3.

239. Dodds (1959) in his commentary (p. 330) (and in the critical apparatus, p. 153) reports a conjecture by Kratz to the effect that νόμος should be replaced by κόσμος or κόσμιον.

240. *Gorgias* 506c 5–e 4.

241. Geometrical equality is the identity between two ratios (a:b = c:d). It is introduced here without explanation, but with the clear implication that it is different from arithmetical equality (a = b). In social terms, the latter implies strictly equal distribution of benefits and duties; the former allows for proportional distribution according to some standard.

242. *Gorgias* 507 e 3–508a 8.

243. *Gorgias* 506e 4–507a 2.

244. Cf. *Gorgias* 508a 4.

245. *Gorgias* 507a 5–c 7.

246. On the question of the essential unity of the virtues (which this passage presents only as a matter of entailment), cf. the studies by Penner, Woodruff, and Ferejohn mentioned in note 9, *supra*.

247. *Gorgias* 506d 1–2.

248. This question only makes sense under the assumption that in the early dialogues (especially in the *Apology* and the *Crito*) Plato was attempting to reconstruct Socrates' ethical thought.

249. The notion of Aristotelian metaphysics has been derived from *Metaphysics* 1. 2. 982 a 19–25; 4. 1. 1003 a 21–26; 6. 1. 1026 a 30–31.

250. Cf. *Metaphysics* 1. 6. 987 b 1–7; 13. 9. 1086 a 37–b 5; 13. 4. 1078 b 17–32; *Parts of Animals* 1. 1. 642 a 24–31. Aristotle distinguishes clearly between the contributions of the historical Socrates and the doctrines held by the Socrates of the dialogues. Although he was born approximately fifteen years after Socrates' death, we should not forget that Aristotle lived for twenty years in Plato's Academy, where he had ample opportunity to obtain information on the Socratic question from Plato himself.

251. Dodds (1959), pp. 336–338, provides arguments to show that these are all Pythagorean notions. The best overall account of Pythagoras and Pythagoreanism is still Burkert (1972). A short critical discussion of the main sources appears in Kirk, Raven, and Schofield (1983), pp. 214–238. On Pythagoras being the first to apply the name "cosmos" to the universe, cf. Aetius 2. 1. 1. and the discussion in Guthrie (1962), pp. 206–212.

252. Guthrie (1971b), p. 52.

253. Cf. Burnet (1911), pp. xliii–xliv, liv–lv.

254. Cf. Grube (1935), pp. 291–294.

255. Cf. Vlastos (1991), pp. 48 and 107–131. According to Xenophon, Socrates even discouraged people from pursuing mathematics beyond the competence needed to measure a parcel of land. Cf. *Mem.* 4. 7. 2–3 and Vlastos (1991), p. 129, n. 96.

256. *Protagoras* 315b 6 ("in an orderly manner") and *Lysis* 205e 2 ("adornment").

257. *Apology* 28e and *Crito* 52b.

258. *Gorgias* 493a 6. Cf. Dodds (1959), pp. 296–299.

259. *Ep. VII* 338c and 350a–b. Cicero believed that Plato went to Italy precisely because he wanted to learn about the Pythagoreans. Cf. *De Fin.* 5. 29. 87; *Rep.* 1. 10. 16; *Tusc.* 1. 17. 39 [referred to by Guthrie (1975), Vol. I, p. 17]. Cf. further Vlastos (1991), pp. 128–129.

260. Cf. Dodds (1959), p. 21, n 3: "What does appear unsocratic, and is candidly marked as a borrowing from another source (507e), is the new 'Platonic' way of describing the Good [*sic*] in terms of 'order' (τάξις,

κόσμος) which is introduced for the first time in the *Gorgias."*

261. If [with Finnis (1980)] we reject the notion that natural law ethics makes inferences from the whole of nature (or from human nature) to moral norms and hold instead that its starting points are axioms that identify basic human goods, then Socrates may well be regarded as its founder.

Conclusion

262. *Gorgias* 495a 5–6.

263. I owe the identification of these passages and the general inspiration for my conclusions to Kahn (1983), pp. 110–111. Cf. Vlastos (1983).

264. *Gorgias* 474b 2–5.

265. *Gorgias* 475e 3–6.

266. *Gorgias* 482b 4–c 3.

267. *Gorgias* 508e 6–509a 7.

268. Cf. *Meno* 77b 6–78b 2.

269. *Gorgias* 505e 6–506a 5.

Appendix

1. The exact nature of the absurdity is obscure and has been much disputed. Cf. Taylor (1976), p. 182.

2. Dodds (1959), p. 21, n. 3.

3. Vlastos (1956), p. xl.

4. Irwin (1977), p. 106. In earlier scholarship, the view that Socrates is seriously upholding hedonistic doctrine was defended by Grote (1875), II. 87–89, and by Hackforth (1928). Cf. also Taylor (1976), p. 209.

5. Vlastos (1991), p. 300.

6. Zeyl (1980) *passim*, esp. pp. 258–259.

7. Cf. Frede (1992), p. xxvii–xxviii.

8. Cf. Kahn (1988a).

9. Cf. Irwin (1977), p. 103.

Index of Principles

(P1) A choice is rational if and only if it is a choice of what is best for the agent.   p. 7

(P2) For every human being, it is good to be a good human being.   p. 8

(P2a) For every human being, the best is to be an excellent human being.   p. 8

(P3) Every agent, in performing an action, should consider *exclusively* whether what he is about to do is just or unjust.   p. 35

(P4) Every agent who has taken a position in the belief that it is for the best ought to remain in his post.   p. 35

(P5) Every agent whose post has been assigned to him by his commanding officer ought to remain in his post.   p. 35

(P6) One should in no way do wrong.   p. 56

(P7) To do wrong is in every way bad and shameful.   p. 56

(P8) The bad and the shameful should not be done.   p. 56

(P9) One should not do wrong in return for having suffered wrong.   p. 57

(P10) Just agreements ought to be fulfilled.   p. 57

(P11) Not life, but the good life, ought to be valued above all else.   p. 68

(P12) The good life is the noble and just life.   p. 68

(P13) Something is good for an agent if and only if it is morally right.   p. 69

(P14) The greatest good, i.e., happiness, consists in noble and good action.   p. 79

(P15) The greatest evil consists in unjust action.   p. 79

(P16) Every agent wants his own real good.   p. 80

(P17) Every agent ought to want his own real good.   p. 80
(P18) A being is good if and only if it has the order proper for it. p. 105

Bibliography

Adkins, A.W.H. (1960). *Merit and Responsibility. A Study in Greek Values.* Oxford.

Allen, R. E. (1960). "The Socratic Paradox." *Journal of the History of Ideas* 21: 256–265.

Allen, R. E. (1972). "Law and Justice in Plato's *Crito.*" *Journal of Philosophy,* 69: 557–567.

Allen, R. E. (1980). *Socrates and Legal Obligation.* Minneapolis. Includes complete translation of the *Apology* and *Crito.*

Amandry, P. (1950). *La Mantique apollinière à Delphes: essai sur le fonctionement de l'oracle.* Paris.

Andronicos, M. (1981). *The Acropolis.* Athens.

Anton, J. P. (1980). "Dialectic and Health in Plato's *Gorgias.*" *Ancient Philosophy* 1: 49–60.

Ashmole, B. (1972). *Architect and Sculptor in Classical Greece.* New York.

Ballard, E. (1965). *Socratic Ignorance: An Essay on Platonic Self-Knowledge.* Den Haag.

Bambrough, J. (1960). "The Socratic Paradox." *Philosophical Quarterly* 10: 289–300.

Barker, A. (1977). "Why Did Socrates Refuse to Escape?" *Phronesis* 22: 13–28.

Barnes, J. (1984). *The Complete Works of Aristotle. The Revised Oxford Translation.* 2 vols. Princeton.

Benson, H. (ed.) (1992). *Essays on the Philosophy of Socrates.* New York.

Bostock, D. (1990). "The Interpretation of Plato's *Crito.*" *Phronesis* 35: 1–20.

Boutroux, E. (1908). "Socrate, fondateur de la science morale," in

Boutroux, *Études d'histoire de la philosophie.* Paris.

Brandwood, L. (1976). *A Word-Index to Plato.* Leeds.

Brandwood, L. (1990). *The Chronology of Plato's Dialogues.* Cambridge.

Brickhouse, T. C., and Smith, N. D. (1989). *Socrates on Trial.* Princeton.

Burkert, W. (1972). *Lore and Science in Ancient Pythagoreanism.* Cambridge (original version: *Weisheit und Wissenschaft.* Nürnberg, 1962).

Burn, A. R. (1966). *The Pelican History of Greece.* Harmondsworth.

Burnet, J. (1900–1907). *Platonis Opera.* 5 vols. Oxford. Standard edition of the Greek text of the Platonic dialogues.

Burnet, J. (1911). *Plato's Phaedo.* Oxford (reprint 1985). Greek text and commentary.

Burnet, J. (1924). *Plato's Euthyphro, Apology of Socrates and Crito.* Oxford. Greek text and commentary.

Burnyeat, M. (1971). "Virtues in Action," in Vlastos (1971), 209–234.

Burnyeat, M. (1977). "Socratic Midwifery, Platonic Inspiration." *Bulletin of the Institute of Classical Studies* 24: 7–16 (reprinted in Benson (1992): 53–65).

Bury, J. B., and Meiggs, R. (1975). *A History of Greece to the Death of Alexander the Great.* 4th ed. New York (reprint 1985).

Calogero, G. (1957). "Gorgias and the Socratic Principle *Nemo sua sponte peccat." Journal of Hellenic Studies* 77: 12–17.

Chroust, A. H. (1957). *Socrates, Man and Myth.* South Bend.

Cohen, M. (1971). "Socrates and the Definition of Piety: *Euthyphro* 10A–11B" in Vlastos (1971), 158–176.

Cooper, J. M. (1975). *Reason and Human Good in Aristotle.* Indianapolis and Cambridge, Mass.

Cornford, F. M. (1932). *Before and after Socrates.* Cambridge (reprint 1982).

Cornford, F. M. (1952). *Principium Sapientiae. The Origins of Greek Philosophical Thought.* Cambridge (reprint Gloucester, Mass., 1971).

Creed, J. L. (1973). "Moral Values in the Age of Thucydides." *Classical Quarterly* 23: 213–231.

Croiset, A. (1920). Platon, *Hippias Mineur, Alcibiade I, Apologie de*

Socrate, Euthyphron, Criton. Paris. Greek text and French translation.

Croiset, A. (1923). Platon, *Gorgias, Ménon.* Paris. Greek text and French translation.

Deman, Th. (1942). *Le Témoignage d'Aristote sur Socrate.* Paris. Selections in Greek and French with commentary.

Diels, H., and Kranz, W. (1956). *Die Fragmente der Vorsokratiker.* 8th ed., Berlin.

Dittmar, H. (1912). *Aischines von Sphettos: Studien zur Literaturgeschichte der Sokratiker.* Berlin.

Dodds, R. E. (1959). Plato, *Gorgias.* Oxford (reprint 1959). Greek text and commentary.

Dover, K. J. (1968). Aristophanes, *Clouds.* Oxford. Greek text and commentary.

Dover, K. J. (1971). "Socrates in the *Clouds,*" in Vlastos (1971), 50–77.

Dover, K. J. (1976). "The Freedom of the Intellectual in Greek Society." *Talanta* 7: 24–54.

Dover, K. J. (1978). *Greek Homosexuality.* Cambridge.

Drexler, H. (1961). "Gedanken über den Sokrates der platonischen *Apologie.*" *Emerita.* 29: 177–201.

Duchemin, J. (1943). "Remarques sur la composition du *Gorgias.*" *Revue des Études Grecques* 66: 265–286.

Dudley, D. R. (1960). *The Civilization of Rome.* New York.

Dupréel, E. (1922). *La légende socratique et les sources de Platon.* Bruxelles.

Dyson, M. (1976). "Knowledge and Hedonism in Plato's *Protagoras.*" *Journal of Hellenic Studies* 96: 32–45.

Ehrenberg, V. (1921). *Die Rechtsidee im frühen Griechentum.* Leipzig (reprint Hildesheim, 1966).

Ehrenberg, V. (1923). "Anfänge des griechischen Naturrechts." *Archiv für Geschichte der Philosophie* 35: 119–143.

Ferejohn, M. T. (1982). "The Unity of Virtue and the Objects of Socratic Inquiry." *Journal of the History of Philosophy* 20: 1–21.

Field, C. G. (1923). "Aristotle's Account of the Historical Origin of the Theory of Ideas." *Classical Quarterly* 17: 113–124.

Field, C. G. (1930). *Plato and His Contemporaries.* London.

Finnis, J. (1980). *Natural Law and Natural Rights.* Oxford.

Flashar, H. (1958). *Der Dialog Ion als Zeugnis platonischer Philosophie.* Berlin.

Flashar, H. (1983). *Aeltere Akademie, Aristoteles, Peripatos.* Vol. 3 of Die Philosophie der Antike in Ueberweg, *Grundriss der Geschichte der Philosophie.* Basel-Stuttgart.

Fontenrose, J. (1978). *The Delphic Oracle.* Berkeley.

Frankena, W. K. (1963). *Ethics.* Englewood Cliffs (reprint 1973).

Frede, M. (1992). Introduction to Plato, *Protagoras.* Trans. by S. Lombardo and K. Bell. Indianapolis and Cambridge, Mass.

Gallop, D. (1964). "The Socratic Paradox in the *Protagoras.*" *Phronesis* 9: 117–129.

Geach, P. (1966). "Plato's *Euthyphro:* An Analysis and Commentary." *Monist* 50: 369–382.

Gigon, O. (1947). *Sokrates: Sein Bild in Dichtung und Geschichte.* Bern (2nd ed., 1979).

Gill, C. (1973). "The Death of Socrates." *Classical Quarterly* 23: 25–28.

Glassen, P. (1957). "A Fallacy in Aristotle's Argument about the Good." *Philosophical Quarterly* 66: 319–322.

Gómez-Lobo, A. (1991). "Philosophical Remarks on Thucydides' Melian Dialogue." *Proceedings of the Boston Area Colloquium in Ancient Philosophy.* Vol. V. Lanham, 181–203.

Gould, J. (1955). *The Development of Plato's Ethics.* Cambridge.

Grote, G. (1875). *Plato and the Other Companions of Sokrates.* 3 vols. 3rd ed. London.

Grube, G.M.A. (1935). *Plato's Thought.* London (reprint Indianapolis, 1980).

Grube, G.M.A. (1981). Plato, *Five Dialogues: Euthyphro, Apology, Crito, Meno, Phaedo.* Indianapolis and Cambridge, Mass. English translation.

Gulley, N. (1965). "The Interpretation of 'No One Does Wrong Willingly' in Plato's Dialogues." *Phronesis* 10: 82–96.

Gulley, N. (1968). *The Philosophy of Socrates.* London.

Gundert, H. (1954). "Platon und das Daimonion des Sokrates." *Gymnasium* 61: 513–531.

Guthrie, W.K.C. (1962). *A History of Greek Philosophy*, Vol. I. The earlier Presocratics and the Pythagoreans. Cambridge (reprint 1980).

Guthrie, W.K.C. (1965). *A History of Greek Philosophy*, Vol. II. The Presocratic tradition from Parmenides to Democritus. Cambridge (reprint 1978).

Guthrie, W.K.C. (1971a). *The Sophists*. Cambridge (reprint 1979).

Guthrie, W.K.C. (1971b). *Socrates*. Cambridge.

Guthrie, W.K.C. (1975). *A History of Greek Philosophy*, Vol. IV. Plato: The Man and His Dialogues: Earlier Period. Cambridge (reprint 1986).

Guthrie, W.K.C. (1978). *A History of Greek Philosophy*, Vol. V. The later Plato and the Academy. Cambridge (reprint 1986).

Hackforth, R. (1928). "Hedonism in Plato's *Protagoras*." *Classical Quarterly* 28: 39–42.

Havelock, E. A. (1934). "The Evidence for the Teaching of Socrates." *Transactions of the American Philological Association*. 65: 282–295.

Heinimann, F. (1945). *Nomos und Physis. Herkunft und Bedeutung einer Antithese im griechischen Denken des 5. Jahrhunderts*. Basel (reprint Darmstadt, 1980).

Hirzel, R. (1907). *Themis, Dike und Verwandtes*. Leipzig (reprint Hildesheim, 1966).

Huby, P. (1967). *Greek Ethics*. London.

Irwin, T. (1979). Plato, *Gorgias*. Oxford. Translation and commentary.

Irwin, T. (1982). *Plato's Moral Theory: The Early and Middle Dialogues*. Oxford.

Irwin, T. (1986). "Socrates the Epicurean." *Illinois Classical Studies* 11: 85–112 (reprinted in Benson (1992): 198–219).

Kahn, C. H. (1981). "Did Plato Write Socratic Dialogues?" *Classical Quarterly* 31: 305–320.

Kahn, C. H. (1983). "Drama and Dialectic in Plato's *Gorgias*." *Oxford Studies in Ancient Philosophy* 1: 75–121.

Kahn, C. H. (1988a). "On the Relative Date of the *Gorgias* and the *Protagoras*." *Oxford Studies in Ancient Philosophy* 6: 69–102.

Kahn, C. H. (1988b). "Plato and Socrates in the *Protagoras*."

Methexis 1: 33–52.

Kahn, C. H. (1992). "Plato as Socratic." *Studi Italiani di Filologia Classica* 10: 580–595.

Kahn, C. H. (1993). "Proleptic Composition in the *Republic,* or Why Book I was Never a Separate Dialogue." *Classical Quarterly* 43: 131–142.

Kerferd, G. B. (1974). "Plato's Treatment of Callicles in the *Gorgias.*" *Proceedings of the Cambridge Philological Society* 20: 48–52.

Kerferd, G. B. (1981). *The Sophistic Movement.* Cambridge.

Kidd, I. G. (1967). Art. "Socrates." *The Encyclopedia of Philosophy.* Ed. P. Edwards. New York. 7: 480–486.

Kirk, G. S.; Raven, J. E.; and Schofield, M. (1983). *The Presocratic Philosophers: A Critical History with a Selection of Texts.* 2nd ed. Cambridge (1st ed., Kirk and Raven 1957).

Kraut, R. (1983). "Comments on Vlastos." *Oxford Studies in Ancient Philosophy* 1: 59–70.

Kraut, R. (1984). *Socrates and the State.* Princeton.

Lacey, A. R. (1971). "Our Knowledge of Socrates." In Vlastos (1971), 22–49.

Lesher, J. (1987). "Socrates' Disavowal of Knowledge." *Journal of the History of Philosophy* 25: 275–288.

Liddell, H. G., and Scott, R. (1953). *A Greek-English Lexicon.* 9th ed. Oxford.

Lledó, E., *et al.* (1981). Platón, *Diálogos I: Apología, Critón, Eutifrón, Ion, Lisis, Cármides, Hippias Menor, Hippias Mayor, Laques, Protágoras.* Madrid. Spanish translation.

Lledó, E., *et al.* (1983). Platón, *Diálogos II: Gorgias, Menéxeno, Eutidemo, Menón, Cratilo.* Madrid. Spanish translation.

Lloyd-Jones, H. (1983). *The Justice of Zeus.* Berkeley. (2nd ed.).

Long, A. A. (1970). "Morals and Values in Homer." *Journal of Hellenic Studies* 90: 121 ff.

Mackenzie, M. M. (1981). *Plato on Punishment.* Berkeley.

Mackenzie, M. M. (1988). "The Virtues of Socratic Ignorance." *Classical Quarterly* 38: 331–350.

McTighe, K. (1984). "Socrates on Desire for the Good and the Involuntariness of Wrongdoing: *Gorgias* 466a–468e." *Phronesis* 29: 193–236.

Magalhães-Vilhena, V. de. (1952). *I Le problème de Socrate: Le Socrate historique et le Socrate de Platon. II Socrate et la légende platonicienne.* Paris.

Maier, H. (1913). *Sokrates: Sein Werk und seine geschichtliche Stellung.* Tübingen.

Marchant, E. C. (1900). Xenophontis *Commentarii, Oeconomicus, Convivium, Apologia Socratis.* Oxford. OCT (reprint 1982). Greek text.

Marchant, E. C., and Todd, O. J. (1923). Xenophon, *Memorabilia, Oeconomicus, Symposium and Apology.* Cambridge, Mass. and London (reprint 1979). Greek text and translation.

Moreau, J. (1978). "La paradoxe socratique." *Revue de Théologie et Philosophie* 110: 269–279.

Morrison, D. R. (1987). "On Professor Vlastos' Xenophon." *Ancient Philosophy* 7: 9–22.

Morrison, D. R. (1988). *Bibliography of Editions, Translations, and Commentary on Xenophon's Socratic Writings 1600–Present.* Pittsburgh.

O'Brien, M. J. (1967). *The Socratic Paradoxes and the Greek Mind.* Chapel Hill.

Ostwald, M. (1956). Plato, *Protagoras.* New York, London (reprint 1988). Translation.

Patzer, A. (1987), ed. *Der historische Sokrates.* Darmstadt.

Peck, A. L., and Forster, E. S. (1937). Aristotle. *Parts of Animals, Movement of Animals, and Progression of Animals.* Cambridge, Mass. and London (reprint 1968). Greek text and English translation.

Penner, T. (1973). "The unity of virtue." *Philosophical Review.* 82: 35–68 (reprinted in Benson (1992): 162–184).

Pfannkuche, W. (1988). *Platons Ethik als Theorie des guten Lebens.* Freiburg.

Praechter, K. (1923). *Die Philosophie des Altertums.* Vol. I of Ueberweg-Heinze, *Grundriss der Geschichte der Philosophie.* Basel (reprint 1960).

Rawls, J. (1971). *A Theory of Justice.* Cambridge, Mass.

Reeve, C.D.C. (1989). *Socrates in the Apology. An Essay on Plato's Apology of Socrates.* Indianapolis and Cambridge, Mass.

Robinson, R. (1941). *Plato's Earlier Dialectic.* Oxford (2nd ed. 1953).

Roochnik, D. L. (1986). "Socrates' Use of the Techne-analogy." *Journal of the History of Philosophy* 24: 295–310 (reprinted in Benson (1992), 185–197).

Ross, W. D. (1924). Aristotle, *Metaphysics.* 2 vols. Oxford (reprint 1953). Greek text and commentary.

Ross, W. D. (1951). *Plato's Theory of Ideas.* Oxford.

Rowe, C. (1976). *An Introduction to Greek Ethics.* London.

Santa Cruz, M. I. (1991). Review of A. Gómez-Lobo, *La Etica de Socrates. Methexis* 4: 139–143.

Santas, G. (1971). "Socrates at Work on Virtue and Knowledge." In Vlastos (1971), 177–208.

Santas, G. (1971a). "Plato's *Protagoras* and the Explanations of Weakness." In Vlastos (1971), 264–298.

Santas, G. (1972). "The Socratic Fallacy." *Journal of the History of Philosophy* 10: 127–141.

Santas, G. X. (1982). *Socrates. Philosophy in Plato's Early Dialogues.* London.

Schmidt, U. (1980). Platón, *Gorgias.* México. Greek text and Spanish translation.

Sommerstein, A. H. (1973). Aristophanes, *The Acharnians, The Clouds, Lysistrata.* Harmondsworth (reprint 1986). English translation.

Sprague, R. K. (1972). *The Older Sophists.* Columbia, S.C.

Stemmer, P. (1992). *Platons Dialektik: Die frühen und mittleren Dialoge.* Berlin.

Stocks, J. L. (1913). "The Argument of Plato, *Prot.* 351A–356C." *Classical Quarterly* 7: 100 ff.

Strycker, E. de. (1971). "Le *Criton* de Platon. Structure littéraire et intention philosophique." *Les Études Classiques* 39: 417–436.

Sullivan, J. P. (1961). "Hedonism in Plato's *Protagoras.*" *Phronesis* 6: 10–28.

Taylor, C.C.W. (1976). Plato, *Protagoras.* Oxford. Translation and commentary.

Tredennick, H. (1954). *The Last Days of Socrates.* Harmondsworth (reprint 1969). Translations of *Euthyphro, Apology, Crito* and *Phaedo.*

Versényi, L. (1963). *Socratic Humanism.* New Haven.

Vlastos, G. (1956). "Introduction." In Ostwald (1956), vii–lvi.

Vlastos, G. (1967). "Was Polus Refuted?" *American Journal of Philology* 88: 454–460.

Vlastos, G. (1969). "Socrates on Acrasia." *Phoenix* 23: 71–88.

Vlastos, G. (1971) (ed.). *The Philosophy of Socrates: A Collection of Critical Essays.* Garden City.

Vlastos, G. (1971a). "The Paradox of Socrates." In Vlastos (1971), 1–21.

Vlastos, G. (1974). "Socrates on Political Obedience and Disobedience." *Yale Review* 42: 517–534.

Vlastos, G. (1983a). "The Socratic Elenchus." "Afterthoughts on the Socratic Elenchus." *Oxford Studies in Ancient Philosophy* 1: 27–58; 71–74.

Vlastos, G. (1983b). "The Historical Socrates and Athenian Democracy." *Political Theory* 11: 495–516.

Vlastos, G. (1984). "Happiness and Virtue in Socrates' Moral Theory." *Proceedings of the Cambridge Philological Society* 30: 181–213 [reprinted with substantial revisions in Vlastos (1991): 200–232].

Vlastos, G. (1985). "Socrates' Disavowal of Knowledge." *Philosophical Quarterly* 35: 1–31.

Vlastos, G. (1991). *Socrates, Ironist and Moral Philosopher.* Ithaca.

Vogel, C. J. de (1955). "The Present State of the Socrates Problem." *Phronesis* 1: 26–35.

Walsh, J. J. (1971). "The Socratic Denial of Akrasia." In Vlastos (1971), 235–263.

Wedberg, A. (1955). *Plato's Philosophy of Mathematics.* Stockholm.

White, A. R. (ed.) (1968). *The Philosophy of Action.* Oxford.

Wilamowitz-Moellendorff, U. von (1919). *Platon: Sein Leben und seine Werke* and *Platon: Beilagen und Textkritik.* 2 vols. Berlin.

Wolz, H. G. (1967). "Hedonism in the *Protagoras.*" *Journal of the History of Philosophy* 5: 205–217.

Woodruff, P. (1976). "Socrates on the Parts of Virtue." *Canadian Journal of Philosophy. Suppl.* 2: 101–116.

Woodruff, P. (1992). "Plato's Early Theory of Knowledge." In Benson (1992), 86–106.

Woozley, A. D. (1971). "Socrates on Disobeying the Law." In Vlastos (1971), 299–318.

Young, G. (1974). "Socrates and Obedience." *Phronesis* 19: 1–29.

Zeyl, D. J. (1980). "Socrates and Hedonism: *Protagoras* 351b–358d." *Phronesis* 25: 250–269.

Zeyl, D. J. (1982). "Socratic Virtue and Happiness." *Archiv für Geschichte der Philosophie* 64: 225–238.

Zeyl, D. J. (1987). Plato, *Gorgias.* Indianapolis. English translation.